DISCARDED

An East Tennessee Nightmare Lying in Wait

Babette Anton

iUniverse, Inc.
New York   Bloomington

An East Tennessee Nightmare Lying in Wait

Copyright © 2008 by Babette Anton

All rights reserved. No part of this book may be used or reproduced by any means, graphic, electronic, or mechanical, including photocopying, recording, taping or by any information storage retrieval system without the written permission of the publisher except in the case of brief quotations embodied in critical articles and reviews.

iUniverse books may be ordered through booksellers or by contacting:

iUniverse
1663 Liberty Drive
Bloomington, IN 47403
www.iuniverse.com
1-800-Authors (1-800-288-4677)

Because of the dynamic nature of the Internet, any Web addresses or links contained in this book may have changed since publication and may no longer be valid. The views expressed in this work are solely those of the author and do not necessarily reflect the views of the publisher, and the publisher hereby disclaims any responsibility for them.

ISBN: 978-0-595-52718-2 (pbk)
ISBN: 978-0-595-51658-2 (cloth)
ISBN: 978-0-595-62769-1 (ebk)

Printed in the United States of America

iUniverse Rev. 12/29/08

An East Tennessee Nightmare Lying in Wait

By Babette Anton

"*Keynote*"

The brothers Houston's years of militia-styled threats and self-styled lawsuits kept citizens on edge. Then there were two dead cops and two jailed Houstons. Was this to be peace in the valley, or a life for a life? Only a trial could decide.

"We cannot escape our dangers by recoiling from them."

- Winston Churchill

Acknowledgments

This book is for the many people who wanted this story to be told and who encouraged me over my two-and-a-half years of research and work. I give particular thanks to Dolly and Dr. E for their earliest insights and faith in me—two of the strongest women I will ever know. I must thank Dr. Randy Dupont at the University of Memphis for steering my knowledge to include culture classes, to Larry and Mary Oran who have cherished and epitomized the best in their family's long Roane County history, and to Mama Mia's Restaurant for keeping me fed. I especially would like to thank my nameless friend who has challenged me for years to put forth a sound argument. And without hesitation I applaud the men and women of law enforcement who live and die as they face off with the lawless. Close to home I want to thank my sons Karl and Thor for their earliest and extended bravery, and for the resulting courage they built in me. Most importantly, I thank my husband who has always been steadfast in his encouragement. This book would not have happened without him. Finally, I salute those who I know and those who I will never know who work to secure a safer, better world.

Contents

Book One   How It Went Down 1
   Community Fears 3
   Roane Beckons 7
   The Hand That Feeds 11
   Ambush Defined 18
   Cop to the Ambush 22
   Man Hunt 28
   Homes within Range 31
   Grew Fat on Kindness 36
   Stockton's New School 41
   Heritage Stands Up 45
   Weapons Win 48
   Resolution to Revolution 51
   Unforgettable Swift Change 55
   The Law Soldiers On 60

Book Two   When They Became the Houstons 65
   A Far Cry from Old Ed Houston 67
   Homebound Boys to Men 71
   Different Game Board 78
   Matched Against the Feds 81
   The Law Unhinged 86
   The Uncompromising Duo 90

Dead Set to Outlast Court *94*
Premeditation before the Court *98*
Halfway There *101*
More than Law Geeks *105*
Court Moves *112*
Serial Drama *116*
Red Flags to Red Flares *120*
Straight Answers *124*
BookThree Trapped in Themselves 127
   Déjà vu Teaches *129*
   The Waco Manifesto *135*
   Wacky to Waco *141*
   Sociopaths in Their Own Heroic Story *144*
   Trained to Kill *151*
   Smoking Them Out *155*
   Government in Their Sights *157*
   Nightmare Speeds On *163*
   Post Script *165*

BOOK ONE

How It Went Down

Chapter 1

Community Fears

What lies in wait for any of us is often fearful, but seldom foreseeable. Plentiful acts of mayhem record themselves but do not always predict the future. Yet in Roane County Tennessee, such bad acts continued and accelerated without solution. For certain, beneath the surface, accumulating nightmarish fear had set in amongst the population. But even such a community's predilection on what might be lying in wait was not enough to stop the fright or the well known transgressors.

Criminal stealth has the upper hand, a hand that actually holds such ideas in place. Only when mayhem turns to murder, do people more comfortably speak out about how they had seen it coming:

Murder stops folks in their tracks. Then suddenly the previous whispered worries create uproar of relief and shock. Prior hidden knowledge makes itself known.

In the alleged double first degree murders of May 11, 2006, the admitted killers Rocky Houston and Leon Houston ended the collected fears. And, for a short time anyway, their terrible swift deeds temporarily had brought peace to the valley. The brothers, having long talked openly about "killing cops," stood true to their word. They killed Roane County Sheriff's Deputy William Birl Jones and his physically disabled buddy Gerald Michael Brown who fatefully patrolled the road in front of the troublesome two's family homestead.

The Houstons' precursory warnings, according to sources close to them, had picked up steam over time. Then, suddenly their semi-shrouded intent to kill leapt out into the evening shade that surrounded the front porch of that two story farmhouse with its pitched roof line. Perhaps the brothers' nearly twenty years of notoriety had forced itself on their decision making. Many citizens understood that the brothers' anger was strung tight, but they didn't know just whose lives were on the line. It is doubtful if the Houstons did. They were definitely wired differently, tighter than they should have been.

In a matter of seconds on that May 11th evening at about 6 pm, the brothers Houston, now ages 45 and 47, let loose their once sheltered intentions to kill. Here the uncertainty of what had lain in wait turned to cold stone reality. Two men lay dead in a county patrol car. Both their bodies and vehicle were splintered by a large number of bullets. Some type of assault weapon must have been used. At least one other gun, a semi-automatic pistol had left bullet casings. Caught off guard by the gruesome scene, law enforcement even could have considered this the work of a fully automatic rifle. "Banana clips" were mentioned, but in either case, both "semi-auto" and "fully auto" guns have magazines and not clips. And such magazines can send out anywhere from 40 to 100 rounds. Importantly here, an AK-47 styled semi-auto weapon allows the shooter to choose each time he pulls the trigger. Such a weapon also allows him to selectively stop. In comparison, the "spray and pray" of the military's fully automatic weapon, describes the shooter's potential inaccuracy and possibly loss of control. Nervousness alone could cause a continuous "spray" of bullets. In the end, both weapons would cause one to be dead. They both would require serious practice.

The press knew something about their string of lawsuits. They had been going on for at least fifteen years. Others believed it had been even longer: If there had been a way to atrophy their heinous behavior such a solution had never showed itself.

Then as crimes evolve, they move from what might be considered surprising to not surprising at all. It is natural to start seeing the end—albeit a dead end. Of course often those all knowing bystanders to murder earlier had put their own safety first and looked the other way, closeting that knowledge and throwing away the key. It's only human. What would one expect of them?

After all, few people want to believe their neighbors are capable of killing another human being. So universally most people sit back and wait for what's coming. For them, there is security in that decision. The rest is up to lawmen. They get paid to risk their lives. To serve warrants. They get paid to die for the rest of us. What a job description that is.

But murder reaches well beyond personal boundaries. History records small disagreements that turn to wars. When anti-government killing takes place in the longest surviving democracy—a country which shows concerns about almost everyone—the bad intent becomes baffling.

Things can be different in East Tennessee. In Roane County's hill tops, just west of Knoxville, an act against government—even an unhinged one—can breathe life into old legends. For here the erstwhile distain for government agents of any kind (but typically revenuers of the past) has not completely passed to that "sweet by and by."

The brothers against government, well known as Rocky and Leon, personally brought that militant attitude up to speed. They and their gaggle of followers, felt justified when they stepped up and killed "the law." Then and there, the feared and favored blood brothers plugged two men multiple times with multiple bullets (as many as 40 plus reported at the scene) right between mountain ridges—right where country music amalgamates such legends and captivates memories of a disappearing culture.

After years of Houston assaults against the government, the aging Leon's and Rocky's blood crimes ignited the population into a quarrel that became hot as a pot on a cast iron stove. Crowds for and against the brothers gathered to take sides and handout bumper stickers. Perhaps this would be scandalous to outsiders, but not to locals. Not there, where feud fences display noisy junk and printed threats to hated neighbors; or, where Tennessee's own United States President Andrew Jackson took a shot in the chest during a duel, but held on to kill the man who got off the first shot.

Behind bars waiting for a trial, the duo watched as some on the sidelines kept the community focused on their newsworthy infamy. Their prolonged private insurgency spread on this way to take on a life of its own. Clearly no one knew what new act the bickering would give birth to. Undeniably, the two dead men's justice had been suspended as their families waited almost voiceless.

As reported a few years prior, the youngest of "the boys" promised bringing a second Waco down on the county. In the end, the tormenting forecast of that wish book looked different than the television coverage of Waco, but only because fewer had died.

The bold homicides of Bill Jones, 53, and Mike Brown, 44, on Barnard Narrows Road, although monstrous and preposterous, cemented divisive perspectives in the Tennessee Valley. The frequent opposing opinions took angry sides, and time stood still as some sunk lower and lower into mistaken hopeful beliefs. But the Houston homicides, stoked by constitutional ignorance and long term anger, were too hot to cool down anytime soon.

The fact remains: by springtime of 2006 something terrible hid in the awakening landscape which sprung forward to betray a large number of good souls who lived there. The resulting calamity successfully eliminated East Tennessee's usual Appalachian spring—a soothing mixture of hazy skies and cool breezes.

Chapter 2

Roane Beckons

Kingston is a jewel of a town, within Roane County which itself was created in 1801. Two distinct buildings beckon: both courthouses. The "old" 1854 courthouse stands just a couple of traffic lights into the center of town, right next to the architecturally similar "new" one built about 1979.

The Emory, Clinch, and Tennessee rivers converge right beyond the center of town to nurture the Watts Bar Embayment. Broad estuaries add to the huge water supply that supports hydroelectric power. Mapsters can quickly point to this prominent landscape because of the three rivers.

Seasonal boaters, water sport enthusiasts and second home owners also know the way to Kingston. They trek to the sprawling county's lakeshores and mountain breezes. But the event of that one particular May evening permanently froze disgust into the minds of many residents and non residents. A lot of that merry month of May seemed anything but merry.

Yet, no one casting an eye from Kingston's network of rivers or its intersection with a cross-country interstate highway would see a town divided. And potential threats to citizens most often came by way of traffic accidents from intruding Interstate 40 where mountain top views plummet like ski slopes to bottom out and connect other state and county highways.

The town's I-40 exit appears quickly to both east and west travelers. If vehicles turn off the I and into Kingston, they often jockey for place as they leave menacing, heavy-laden trucks powering down on them off those hill tops. There the trucks depend on downhill momentum to propel them over the opposing upside of the mountains ahead.

So, entering or just riding by, an outsider to this idyllic setting would never expect anyone within the landscape beyond to be guilty of harassing the "Feds." Nor could they guess that a pair of rural brothers had turned a long term war with Knoxville's United States District Court into a deadly assault.

Speculation would have it that as the Houstons' ersatz lawsuits failed them, they returned to their home base to muster support and attack a less formidable army of local enemies. Benefits to this decision accumulated. Putting many of their nuisance lawsuits aside temporarily at least, they returned to spreading tall tales of law enforcement's persecution of them as individuals and others who lived within the borders of their rambling family compound. They wanted to be their own judge and jury.

Apparently, they correctly surveyed their options. Returning their project to local law enforcement put them back in the fight that they had lost for years in Knoxville. They were wrong if they believed they could blindside Roane County's law enforcement establishment, attorneys, and judges. Each group recognized the Houstons' past criminal intent and acknowledged the difficulties of dealing with the heavily armed trouble makers. Aching for attention as anarchists, the Ten Mile two wanted to be recognized. Seen with their high powered rifles in bandoliers across their shoulders and chests, with cocky militia camouflage to boot, they let their dress code speak for them.

A portion of the homefolks believed in Rocky and Leon, regardless of what Sheriff David Haggard on the scene had seen as the brothers' ambush murders. Hardly expected, a collection of followers felt that the twosome only did what they had to do. To some, the loss of two lives seemed a fair exchange for anyone who dared to come looking for them. The only victims in these individuals' minds were the "boys"—definitely not the men they killed. At first, there seemed to be surprisingly vocal number of voices who expressed themselves proportionally for and against the brothers Houston. In their dastardly crime, they got more attention than any benevolent public personality.

Those "for" the Houstons joined in alliance to agree that "the law," or anyone else who drove by their "Ten Mile" home on Barnard Narrows Road deserved to be shot: warrant server or sightseer. That message picked up speed as it spread. In that state of mind, someone might have suggested a warning to read: "Detour: Dangerous Men Ahead." Of course, level headed citizens could not grasp the situation. An educated perception of law and order was flat out missing among the Houston posse.

Clearly, those chosen to stand against the lawless knew an entirely different fact-based scenario. They knew they were dealing with anarchists' moves, but had yet to convince a certain alien population within the boundaries of several East Tennessee counties that the "boys" were not mistreated heroes.

Apparently, ample people in the Houston corner needed a short course in the United States Constitution and a reason to abide by it. Such constitutional understanding evidently meant seeing things according to Rocky and Leon. Getting to know what they were about would require the interpretation of gibberish. Simply put: they meant to eliminate that which they couldn't control by breaking the law

As the "assassination" news spread, the community heard that these homegrown men had "ambushed" a sheriff's patrol. Meaningfully, Rocky and Leon were known on a first name basis among East Tennessee media sources. As before, they made the broadcast and print news. Journalists too had had fearful face-to-face contacts with them—crazed and threatening when the media wouldn't see things their way. What else? Once they made the news, they wanted the news to go their way. As firebrands, they wanted their anti-government conspiracy theories and propaganda delivered.

None to charitable to their heritage, they never shied from maligning their own antecedents. Not many men could commit an assault rifle slaughter right off the wrap-around porch of their family's own noted homestead. Who could believe a home with a Tennessee porch motif staged what was seen as an ambush slaying of two men which, similar only at a glance, is represented by a restaurant franchise that provides front porches filled with inviting rocking chairs? Incongruously, the Houston porch fronted as a crime scene.

Now committing ghastly crimes is one thing. Bringing the shame and notoriety home to those related but uninvolved—both living and dead—is downright self-absorbing and cruel. Yet, changing others lives in order to satiate one's merciless purposes is nothing new in crime circles. In fact, getting an observer's arms around the crime might first expose the long truth behind the blood brothers' frustrated self-images. Everything at the crime scene that evening spoke of plenty of brutal spent rage.

That rage had driven their cause for what began to feel like eternity. Mr. and Mr. Houston never were timid about espousing what they believed was top drawer personal knowledge: According to their never ending lawsuits, corrupt local, state, and national government invested man hours to plot against them. On the face of the accusations, none of it made sense. But, without shame, they repeatedly registered their feverish complaints, roamed the news outlets, and drew negative attention to themselves.

As it goes, they went from being known to being well known. The catch here: the longer that behavior went unchecked, the more anger and less vulnerability they seem to have felt.

Yes, loyalties to outlaws who defied civilized law and order were quite out of place in East Tennessee's beautiful lake area. These harsh incongruities between the two men and their environment thrust themselves onto the scene like the plague.

The community had long known something was lying in wait. And during those fearful years they lost a piece of civil order and freedom. These quarrelsome men had made part of the county map South of the Tennessee River theirs! That "domestic tranquility" so insured constitutionally had been maimed and removed from that part of the county by the brothers Houston and their associates.

Dead set on spreading their venom, they determined to extend their boundaries North of the River. After all it is said that they spent a lot of time in Harriman where Rocky finally blew a traffic whistle on his own bad intentions: yes, speeding in a school zone and yelling out the threat of "Waco" in a courtroom are callous companions. The two say a lot about anyone willing to do either.

The most frightening question remained: Why had these men who salivated for a cruel and violent government "of and by the Houstons" lasted so long? Such insurrectionists lived in other cultures and other countries; right?

Chapter 3

The Hand That Feeds

Remembered for its one day stint as the state's capital in 1807, Kingston is also home to an early Tennessee Valley Authority power plant and serves as a bedroom community to Oak Ridge, known worldwide for the Oak Ridge National Laboratory. The "lab's" earliest reputation was born there with the development of the Atomic Bomb. During that period top secrets and top scientists led to the bomb's completion and its use to end the war.

Some sixty years later it seems a quirk of fate to parallel the ongoing dissent with two down home country boys' distaste for their government. No intellectual war exists either: neither of the brothers proposes thoughtful arguments, which perhaps could be more likely expected from an Oak Ridge scientist, engineer, or even a local official.

Instead those who have kept it going for more than a decade are brotherly combatants. They repeatedly have presented dueling documents that they believe stand firm as lawsuits. Perhaps less comprehensible is fact that the United States Department of Energy for fifteen years had signed one brother's (Rocky's) paycheck. Professionally, he was a security guard.

The homicides, perpetrated by Rocky and Leon Houston (with no profession or obvious employment history), most definitely were entangled in their hatred of government and lawyers. Self-appointed lawyers or not, they fought the rule of law. They scorned its clear-cut distinctions. In contrast, many citizens took exception to their attitude and feared their actions.

For what seemed like ages, onlookers saw the brothers Houstons' behavior pointing towards potential kill'ns.

Who could miss their abrasive loud opposition? Gentlemen farmers they were not. Their forbearers had been; but Rocky and Leon made that so easy to forget. They had turned themselves into argumentative public nuisances. If the public had a say in the bottom line, the Houstons were rabble rousing roughens who long prior to their most dastardly act had bitten the hand that fed them:

Indirectly and directly their own lives had enjoyed the gifts of time. They and their family had benefited from the modernity which T.V.A. brought to their distressed area prior to their own births. The federally owned utility brought electrical power to a region that long had languished behind the industrial states to the north. Not to be missed either was Rocky Houston's long term employment with the United States Department of Energy.

Benefits aside, the often agitated and frenzied brothers courted a dark vision. Their self-styled lawsuits show that cobwebs of laddered conspiracy theories filled their minds, eventually believing officials across America plotted to take their lives. Without slackening their anti-government diction, according to confidants, they went forward to to speak about silencing those they believed conspired against them. For a long while it was just mud throwing that wouldn't stick. Definitively, life to them was not a gift given that couldn't be taken.

Quite innocently it would seem that Deputy Jones and his friend Brown (medically retired from the law) paid with their lives because of two other men's reliable rashness and unidentifiable mental states: The reported twisted mental intrigue working on their minds must have driven them to uphold their boastful goals of "killing a few cops." By this time they could have been merely looking at saving face.

Minds can be the most dangerous things: The brothers Houston had talked the talk but not walked the walk. They could go forward to the finish and accomplish two things: stand behind their word "to kill" and retain front page picture poses. Thoughtfully drilled, and waiting for a crime of opportunity with a few friends on hand, the Houston brothers recognized the predictable: The county patrol would pass their houses. Three shifts each day patrolled the county's lower southeast section. The Houston homestead where they gathered May 11th was as close to the road as any house could be.

Pumped up, their perpetually unhinged mindscapes took charge. They must have been waiting for an opportunity they couldn't pass up. Then and there it appeared: So as the deputy in the marked patrol vehicle drove by and beyond their home to the east, they took it as a taunt. After Jones and

Brown had been killed, who else was talking? Then too, it usually takes an investigator to discern a true motive.

With enough time to watch and wait, they told their friends on the porch to scram. The county patrol went out to guard and protect against those looking for trouble. That's how sheriffs' deputies work everywhere. Alert to suspicious signs they turn around to put a stop to it if they can. When the anti-establishment brothers saw the lawman turning around back toward their porch, they lifted their weapons and secured their battle-ready trigger fingers. They had by now gone on the offensive. They were ready for the second pass. They definitely did not retreat into the farmhouse.

From hidden positions, as suggested by the evidence, they hailed the county vehicle and the two men inside with what was reported to be gun fire from semi-automatic and automatic weapons. Both men fought back as only men realizing their deaths tend to do. Right off the front porch, the sins against man and nature took their toll. In this case at least one of the brothers was a tree hugger in an illegitimate sense of the expression. In motions hearings prior to a trial, the defense claimed Leon had taken a "defensive position" behind a tree. Creating doubt is what defense lawyers are supposed to do. No defense lawyer would do it differently. A prosecutor is not held to that standard. They must provide evidence not doubt to prove their cases to a jury. Getting a jury would be a battle in itself. It would take the utmost care.

The pair's actions lent plenty of faith to the community's long nightmare. True to Rocky's and Leon's mostly irrational choices, their victims were lent no mercy. That routine patrol had vexed them into action. Turning the Ten Mile two's minds inside out, a person might see this as murder by the book: The said they would do it; they did it; they denied it by claiming they were only defending themselves. No problem; once charged, every criminal needs a defense. What more did they have?

No one would argue that this style of retaliation was speedier than their not-so-mighty or swift lawsuits which consistently failed them. Taking a few steps inside during the time lapse of the patrol's turn around was not what they did. Time was of the essence and a factor. Enough time was left on the clock to get their companions safely away from the gunfire, but it also sheds light on their premeditation. Law dictionaries everywhere define premeditation as "forethought for a length of time no matter how short that time may be." Providing a spotless uncorrupted trial would of course be left to the maneuvering of the prosecution and defense. Motion hearings worked with the vibrating possibilities while Judge James (Buddy) Scott worked towards that goal. That takes time. And in the case of most criminals, their applause can be counted on when going forward if they can provide "motions to postpone." Rocky and Leon Houston by July 14, 2008 had been held in area lockups for two years and two months. No one listening to their complaints about their facilities, health care, or even tooth brushes doubted that they wanted out of jail sooner than later.

Vengeance like venom is held in until it spews forward. Sometimes it is waylaid until the time is right. Sometimes it is even forgotten. The Houston duo picked off low level enemies. It was time. They were the easiest game. They knew they never would have the Tennessee governor or United States' President drive by, although they had included them on their list of those conspiring against them and their family members. Their position off their porch could be best illustrated as similar to that of hunters sitting in a duck blind.

Another attempt perhaps at getting to the truth requires looking from the outside into the two Ten Mile residents' minds. It could be that this act of vengeance against these low level enemies brought them temporary solace. Pleasure can come from causing pain to others. Those charged with bringing the country boys in never heard a word of remorse from them. Their angry minds awash in foul moods couldn't make a right turn. With conspirators plotting against them, what was a fellow to do?

After the fact, the bodies of their dead victims were first reported to have taken 67 combined rounds. That early number didn't matter since there was no doubt overkill. As the defense and prosecution traded their own shots in the pre-trail hearings, the number varied. The argument rested when it came down to the essentials: Jones' and Browns' bodies, with their earthly recognition missing, lay just feet from the Houston door step. Instantly, these two guys had gone from being father, husband, brothers, sons, nephews and friends to mutilated humans with a resemblance to Swiss cheese. Billy Jones and Mike Brown were dead and gone at the end of the day. There had been no restraint.

Little doubt that these two dead men paid for Houston pain with their lives. Anger in some way or other seems to ignite every crime. Usually it is seen as a motive. Psychologists claim anger can replace depression. Both of those choices seem possible, but paralyzing ugly.

The bloodied spot in the road, known years ago as Houston Hollow, had claimed the departed. Perhaps some there continued to recognize it as Houston country, although it never had been: It always had been God's country.

With law enforcement everywhere looking for the missing shooters, others stood guarding the crime scene. Strange. Even that spot in the road was temporarily lifted from the anger of the incident itself. Perhaps these rescued moments were a gift given to those left to sort things out. It definitely wasn't man's love for his fellow man that suggested itself to those gathered at the scene.

As recalled, a serene universe settled over the roadside carnage. Nature, for a moment, reached to temporarily veil this forested spot in the Tennessee Valley. Canopied entrances from other connecting country roads and the pitched heights of close ridge tops embraced the recent history with solemnity.

In a sense, time stood still at 6:12 p.m. Many hearts would never beat the same again, with those the officers faced not beating at all. A throng of vehicles responded to the "officer down" call; but those early law enforcement witnesses knew there was nothing they could do to change things. Yet that change was there.

Another presence reached to the loss that lay before them. Jones and Brown, with the breath of life so recently expunged from them, remained positioned as they died. The deputy sat slumped over in the driver's seat of the patrol car, and his "ride along," in an attempt to escape, was seen flung through his open door onto the road with his feet still within the car, reported pasted to the road dying while additional rounds must have flown into his head to make him dead. But these first responders, shaken but focused, saw and felt shafts of light move in to more gently stage the bodies.

An eerie presence reached out to the first witnesses. Some describe it as an unearthly but abiding awkwardness. Clearly, the awkwardness is tantamount to the men's last private, but now public, moments in time.

Kingston Police Chief Jim Washam offers his steady memory to that place in time: "Standing at the scene, a chill covered the road." The chief, himself bound for years to the possibility of this crime scene and those who perpetrated it, recalls the particulars. He talks about the atmosphere which had been whipped up by the cold evening air. He remembers that as a haze descended into this nexus of merging valleys, it seemed to purposely slow as it settled on the dead zone. His description portrayed the night air as it moved with a whisper through the downed vehicle's multiple bullet holes. And together there, the lawmen joined in regret and talked about the attack they already had termed an ambush.

Just before when Constable Butch Barding heard the cacophony of sirens heading into his district, he said he almost knew that this involved the Houstons. He couldn't help tearing up as he covered the deceased faces. Knowing the dead and those accused now missing from the scene, he saw deep into the circumstances; and, he felt the pain of all the families.

The lawyers, the judges, the general population that also knew the Houston saga did not need to witness this conclusion. Those of the Barnard Narrows' Houston families, just a stone's throw away from this havoc, stayed behind closed doors. But one brave member, driving up on the scene, called it in. Each in some way knew what was coming. The Jones' and Brown' relatives quickly would know as well that the worst had happened.

Even those at the scene knew the crime was lying in wait, or at least they knew they had little control of what had been a promise made and kept now. It had been on their minds and other knowledgeable people's for a long time. That definitely put the whole nightmare into a range of predictable violence. They all wished it had been preventable.

Loud raving Rocky and brooding Leon drove themselves to act out their threat against the law. They had talked too often and people heard it. Preferring to be safe in their anonymity, those who asked not to be identified saw the ego-centered brothers as men literally besieged with uncommon and nonsensical fury.

Retired Roane County investigator Clarence Robbins straight out claimed "it didn't have to happen." He believed the predictable could have been preventable. A chorus intoned the same belief. They said that Bill Jones and Mike Brown did not have to die. Most law enforcement thinks the same. In this case the possibilities were up for grabs.

Another covertly organized and gathered SWAT operation could have brought the Houstons in and put them behind bars for their last episode with the Tennessee Forestry Department. They didn't. But there was an active warrant outstanding against Rocky at the time of the homicides.

Now a neighboring man had been convicted of shooting at TVA officers who were clearing property of marijuana which was located not on his property but on property across from his own. The news had it that he had gotten a life sentence out of that behavior.

Clyde Houston, the men's father, thought differently than the law had about the treatment of his grown sons. But he definitely felt he had been given a gift to see them survive alive. Once a Roane County Commissioner respected by many, he defended the two with the belief that law enforcement had "…pushed [them] just too far" Other comments, in disagreement with his, hastily followed: they saw the brutality as an overkill.

Roane County couldn't present itself on a picture postcard for awhile—not this season for sure. The purists saw their Appalachian spring in shambles. Customarily May in East Tennessee speaks well for Mother Earth. By May she has turned her back on winter and quickly constructed spring rains and rainbows. People within this mountainous landscape can applaud the change. They are happy to bury the short term memory of snowfalls and freezes, for they need to get out from under winter's gray overcast skies which can hold a population hostage in melancholy.

And predictably Dogwood trees seem to appear on cue to lead this celebration from April to May. A stage setting only God has assigned to his faithful companion Mother Nature. Suddenly, an apparition steps forward to walk into a spring spectacle of vibrant life. She wears bridal lace made of flower petals that have cascaded down from the Great Smokey Mountains to wed the surrounding hilltops and valleys to life's renewal. Knoxville, home to the University of Tennessee, hosts the main event. There the annual Dogwood Arts Festival regales both those traditional events of April and the promises of May.

Tennessee's "Bible belt" favors folk lore and spring rituals in keeping with the Dogwoods' calendar appearance and the observance of the Easter season. Such deep and sacred roots carry embedded meaning within the Dogwood blossom motif.

According to that faith centered belief, the bloom's four white petals form the shape of a cross. Christ's crown sets within the golden center. The story has it that this snowy white cross retained that image until God gave his son Jesus Christ in death to save men's souls. At that point, Christ's blood flowed to the four pedaled edges, leaving its borders permanently rimmed in red. And that is the face today of every Dogwood blossom.

One must add that nature's spring gateway and Roane's Christian principles brought tears to those witnesses who stood on the Barnard Narrows' roadside crime scene. Soul saving would definitely be turned over to a higher power. The bright hope of the season and May's welcome gestures were stymied. Temporarily time turned to stone. Two pitiless men, according to what witnesses saw, had waited to pounce on the lives of two others.

Those alleged at the time to have carried out crimes had broken the Sixth Commandant many times over. Prominently fortifying that Christian position, the Calvary Baptist Church School's fence posts the Ten Commandments off the I-40 exit as it enters Kingston. No question, those instructions are meant for both the community and wayfarers.

Defiantly the Houstons battered their own Christian code and Appalachia's annual flowering symphony. The highest court of appeal, understood by most there, was not going to be an earthly one.

Chapter 4

Ambush Defined

The sheriff said it was an ambush. Now who would know better? Sheriff David Haggard had been the sheriff for over twelve years in May of 2006. He knew outlaws. He believed he knew the Houstons.

Ambush killings take on a particular significance: They are remembered often in sundry tales of the Old West, once presented at their best in "Living Technicolor." Vivid ambushes played out "in the day" across bloodied American theatre screens in every town in America. And audiences went wild over them. That excitement came to a peak when those lying in wait attacked. Most often they were the winners. Home Box Office television has recently heralded some of these Old West battles.

Political correctness was not yet to be assessed in early Western films. Those movies portrayed battles between American Indians and the United States Cavalry. The term "Native Americans" hadn't been discovered by the public and would have confused them. But they knew what side they were on back then.

Vicarious thrills captured those audiences. Oh to be able to retaliate against those scalp-taking Indians! Although rather one-sided, the films approached what are now known as Native Americans as merciless killers; and so it was. Time took care of the prejudice involved. Such film history then marked the minds of the young and the old population alike. Cowboys and Indians battled on the screen as they presumably did across the early nation.

Consequently, most Americans know how to define an ambush. They know it is bad to be surprised by one. Arrows and bullets fly as one side or the other rides into a trap. The enemy always drew them there, or at least knew their habits well enough to know when and where to lie in wait to ambush them. Children held tight to their breath during those Saturday matinees.

Kids sat on the edge of their seats so focused that they loosened the grip on their popcorn. And as they anticipated the bloodshed, the popcorn spilled and their eyes bugged out. Of course they always recovered. They knew before hand the direction the film's outcome would take: The soldiers would win. They loved it and the outcome.

In truth the cavalry didn't always win like they did on the screen. An example of such was the case of General George Armstrong Custer. Indeed, the General and those who rode with him were killed when the Indians ensnarled them in an ambush. History labeled the horror of this massacre as "Custer's Last Stand." The fact of it was hard to abide. Hardly anyone loved it.

And there was nothing to love about the Barnard Narrows' outcome. Two men rode into those "narrows'" but never rode out. Just like Custer. The human breath taken here didn't resume in minutes as it did to the movie audiences. Jones' and Brown's lives and voices were forever silenced. They didn't live to tell their side of the short, one-sided shootout which looked so much like a trap.

The Barnard Narrows' admitted killers and audience claimed they and a few visitors were sitting back enjoying a snack and a respite when all of this played out. Seconds later they were gone, as were their visitors. Two had been the shooters. They never denied it. They had witnesses too who came in after the fact, just as the brothers Houston did. Uncle Ray Johnson was there, then he wasn't there, then he had them both in the car, then he put Leon out so he could run, and then he took Rocky to the Oak Ridge Medical Center's emergency room. Ray was never charged. Some said he meant well. Roane County treated him well. It has always been a pretty good place to commit a crime.

Most knew there had been more than Ray. Houston friends, to include a couple women, were there. But most of what they had to say and who they were would have to wait 'til trial. Perhaps these women should have been held as conspirators before the fact. They definitely changed their stories as time went by according to those close to the investigation. One Mildred Anne Watts' name came out in the months just before trial. She seemed to be a witness out of nowhere. She was a witness who it seemed couldn't nail down a reliable story. If anything, she just added mystery to the possibilities of "the women on the porch." Other rumors abounded. Fundamentally, those named were all close to the Houston clan.

According to that testimony the Houston porch crew was a late-lunch bunch. But they acted as sentinels when they announced that the marked unit was turning around to make another pass by the Houston house.

The sheriff's patrol knew an active warrant was outstanding against Rocky for which as usual, he had failed to appear. And Deputy Jones was authorized to carry weapons—yes, even the shotgun which Jones is said to have had in the back of his car. Shotguns are standard auxiliary weapons in most police departments. They just are. And they don't do much good out of reach when a man is up against the heavier firepower reported. He would have worn a vest. He didn't. He didn't because it was reported to be in the trunk with "plenty of other," but empty, guns.

Removing Tennessee Forestry firefighters from the property at gunpoint had been the blood brothers' last recorded offense. A deputy unafraid to deal with unstable tyrants stepped up. There they were and there he was.

Insights into the Houstons come through their lawsuits: a great place to investigate since writing professes to be a blueprint of one's mind. Within this drift of written thinking, the brothers Houston often tout their personal admiration for the courage of United States soldiers in Iraq. Why their thinking took them there is left up for grabs. But Bill Jones, a Vietnam veteran who had served his country both as a United States Marine and Army Airborne Ranger was not their kind of combatant. He was uncomfortably different from the Houstons. Veteran Jones fought for his government and against its enemies versus becoming an enemy against his government.

In a probable cause hearing, the men's uncle, Ledford (Ray) Johnson, seems to have unknowingly provided premeditation evidence. He said in an early motion hearing that Leon asked him to leave about eight minutes prior to the hellish outcome. He did. He himself appears to be a bit culpable here. Although Johnson retreated into his nearby home as advised, Mr. and Mr. Houston did not retreat the few steps it took to enter Leon's residence from its porch. The Tennessee Law, at that time, demanded it. They, nor Uncle Ray, nor the other porch friends call the sheriff's department to document their concerns.

They could have complained of what they perceived as harassment. Why not? Their harassment complaints had always been forthcoming before. But then why would they complain how the sheriff's patrol had passed and was turning around? Not one of them would have said that they knew shots would be fired. Not many criminals call in the law on themselves. Some do. They are known as informants.

Instead, in the spirit of the thing, the bystanders only alerted the brothers that the patrol had turned around to come back, according to their witnesses. Perhaps waiting behind cover Rocky and Leon concealed their positions and hunkered down and waited for their prey. Perhaps they were even concealed when the patrol first drove by. There would have been multiple ways to alert them as they first entered Houston Hollow. It could have gone like this:

Forewarned, at least at the car's turn around, the men waited. Large trees and bushes sufficiently surrounded the home and much of the porch. Investigators believed the Houstons leaped, paramilitary style, with guns a blazing. Although Rocky took fire in the hip area (later diagnosed at an internal site as well), Leon wasn't touched in this face off. So interesting!

In effect, the people on the porch appear to have helped mount the killings. Focused facts see them as ancillary participants. Originally, those women and Uncle Ray came forward to give the details of the shoot-to-kill welcoming committee. Then reports, according to early sources, went forth that they, the same people, later recanted much of their testimony, or constantly switched it up. Apparently they never drew the immediately "go to jail" card as accessories this way. Their own guilt drifted just beneath the surface. Perhaps even they feared their compatriots and neighbors.

Stories told will remain for years to come as old time county investigator Clarence Robbins promised. Eventually the Houstons' story will be seen for the ambush which facts document. Jones and Brown just died doing what more and more cops do each year while serving and protecting the constitution's promise to "establish justice."

In the end it is doubtful if the deceased men had completely understood the possible causation behind the brothers Houston's behavior: Like other anti-government groups sprinkled across American, the brothers must have identified with such similar and pervasive underground notions of justice. Much of this group behavior went to filing bogus liens and lawsuits and trying their political opponents on paper. Basically each revolutionary group pushed its alternative legal system and taught it to others. According to years of published media updates in the press and online, their extended philosophies believed (and believe) they one day could replace the nation's justice system with one of their liking.

Chapter 5

Cop to the Ambush

According to military experts asked and *The U.S. Army Doctrine*, ambushes prevail. Lessons go like this: In a classic scenario, someone or something will lure the enemy to the area. Then, another person (or persons) stands as a lookout. The lookout waits to warn of the approaching enemy. Then any number of people may run (commit) the ambush. The limit should be two.

Tactically it is called an L-shaped ambush. Anyone can master the idea with an army manual and time to practice. It might be planned by two people or many people. One person is at the angle of the L—usually to front the attack (waiting for a vehicle); now the second person jumps out to attack from the side. This shooter lets go. The other stationary man keeps the* target pinned in place. Quickly the shooter to the side finishes by moving around the objective, throwing out bullets as he continues. He should finish on the other side of the vehicle, as apparently he did. This takes place in a "killing zone."

For a fact, the act began and ended for Jones and Brown in the "killing zone" by many who perceived it as an ambush. Known also as the "target area," it is chosen ahead to mark the spot where the enemy is expected to pass by. The place, as recorded by military texts, is secured for the assault. Waiting is the game.

No questions stand on whether or not this third shift sheriff's patrol was the Houston's enemy. That was well known. A hatred motive went beyond the third shift itself to its assigned deputy. That man, Bill Jones, was an icon of law enforcement. He was the man you trusted to be there if you needed him. But unlike others, his immediate job meant that he began his daily trip around 3 p.m. He patrolled the southern most region of Roane. That was his duty.

Jones was quite the cop, according to those who worked beside him. These reports say he was a "cops' cop." Harriman Police Chief Jack Stockton (soon to be elected sheriff himself) portrayed him that way. If there was someone bad out there, he was going to go after them.

Jones had been Stockton's training agent. But watch out! There was more. Jack Stockton as Harriman chief in 2001 wrote the letter (required by law) in Rocky's incident of the same year, causing the boisterously wild man's employer to fire him. And yes, more waited. Just prior to May 11, 2006, there was another core connection: Stockton was positioned in the upcoming August 2006 election to become the next Roane County Sheriff.

Rocky and Leon knew all of this. There even had been another candidate's sign on Houston property. Stockton's race must have wound them up a bit. And they were definitely wound differently, according to those who knew them and reported their up close and personal characteristics.

In reality they abhorred Stockton (...so Jones) and Haggard. Both Stockton and Haggard had been sued multiple times in their illusory lawsuits. Not Jones. But it was Sheriff Haggard they kept in their sites. They ranted about him. The marked Roane County deputy's car might as well have had the Haggard and Stockton names splashed across it. So to speak, the men they killed were simply Haggard's and Stockton's messengers.

In an area where duck hunting off the coves of the three connecting rivers is legendary, decoys are just part of the lore of a kid's early life. If Jones realized their rumored fire power was waiting for him behind cover, he never would have turned back. He knew he could not match it. But, if he thought a return trip would just be part of a routine surveillance, he would have gone back to look. Perhaps only the women were standing there where they could be seen. Chatting them up might help him put more faces and information to the renegade group's activities. After all, and after the fact, it was learned that Rocky and Leon had depended on their guests to announce the vehicle's turn around. Where were the brothers grim during that first pass? Was one of them already out front? From the beginning, it looked like the only witnesses to the bloody event would be friends of the Houstons. In this case Rocky and Leon contradicted the adage that "you can run but you can't hide." They had done it so often they had become specialists at running and hiding.

The men's lawyers while they lasted, Randy Rogers and James Logan, said the brothers were just defending themselves against the law. Well, the opposing theory says the Houston already had scripted their positions, which would allow them to conceal themselves and initiate an ambush.

Of course the most important part of the ambush is to be hidden. That would be the Houstons. And of course the marked car was hardly hidden, but in fact a target, as it rode into the valley of death. Standard thinking trains police to see a life threatening situation. No one is advised to let the aggressor fire the first shot.

In the case of Bill Jones, it was his side of the car; his look. Momentarily he would have been thinking of killing the bad guys. He knew that he and Mike Brown didn't have a chance. Experts explain that if caught in this inhospitable position, one immediately attacks the ambush. No cop would choose a defensive position seated within an easy-to-penetrate vehicle, where bullets mushroom as they enter first the car's thin skeletal framework and then into the human targets themselves. Those men in the patrol car were sitting ducks with no escape.

Legally and morally they would have been justified for shooting in any sequence. If threatened by the Houstons or their maneuver, it could have been the cops who should have gotten off that first shot. Cops are taught to be watchful of behavior surrounding or in recognition of their presence. This knowledge of police presence most often means a uniformed officer(s) in a marked car. Those circumstances are firm. And at this point the officer is to give a verbal command or to take charge if possible. Yes, even in an ambush!

Looking back eliminates the question of who shot first from any solid argument. The multiple circumstances add up to a huge Houston offensive. If law enforcement had been undercover the circumstances might have produced a viable discussion for the defense. That is not how it went down.

Picture a man with his automated blistering rifle zeroed in on you. Then in a split second the bupupupup.bpppppppppp.bupppp as he began to unload his magazine into you. In the end that first shot theory meant nothing. It came forth from the defense in the typical requirement to "do something" for your clients in court. But in the slimmest of possibilities that Jones could have or would have shot first, it doesn't attach to the Houstons defending themselves. It wouldn't matter in time whether either brother jumped out from the porch, behind a tree or stood behind one: They ensnared their victims in their trap. The brooding brothers were where they shouldn't have been: hidden and waiting. Little doubt accompanied the forthcoming information that one gun, under these circumstances, would be the choice of a potential assassin. Both men illegally chose positions outside of their home. With plenty of time to see Jones and Brown turn around, they had plenty of time to retreat a few steps into the house. Their friends, told to leave the porch, had time to leave.

The need never existed to know who had shot first. Forensics held the scene tightly in place. Heroically you fire when ambushed whether or not it is first or second. The end result is certain: The men in the car were outgunned by men lying in wait with much more powerful weapons and opportunity.

In the past Rocky said he outran the law because he needed to get home to "people he could trust"—to help him of course. This game of hide-at-home brought the law into his lair and supplied witnesses who would give support to his story. How well that worked on May 11.

Their late afternoon picnic fare doesn't spell out innocent or desirable to many: Just how enticing can the camaraderie of Vienna Sausages and chocolate milk really be? Picture the contradiction of a boxed lunch in one hand and the automatic weapon reported in the other.

Several of their own conspiracy theorists defended the two brothers chosen dress code: They explained that the "boys" carried guns and donned camouflage because they were hunters. Forget it. No big buck deer would be lured from its habitat hungry for canned goods and chocolate. Then too, the idea of a hunter carving a lead riddled venison roast would be ridiculous and comic. The described motive they later produced for the porch crew left a lot out. Yet it might sound good to a jury: Their picnic sounded wholesome enough. But maybe they borrowed their model from a similar homespun practice of "supper on the [church] ground." Whatever their thinking, it took a lot to get in behind it. Most likely it became a patented ruse and offered to their lawyers as part of their courtroom defense.

A real in depth analysis would require assessing the possibility of an even earlier Houston alert. Investigators dig to tie together opportunity, motive and evidence. If the opportunity had played out in the Houston minds, then what would have provided an even earlier opportunity than the designated and described two passes past the porch? Were there lookouts, phone messages, police scanners, text messages, flags, or homing pigeons which let them know the patrol was close and headed their way?

Kingston's Gail Brown reported in July of 2006 that a witness at popular Rocky Top Market on East Race Street (also Highway 70) in Kingston said that Bill Jones had bragged there before heading out on patrol that he was "going down to get the Houstons."

If there was talk there, then who knows what big ears would have contacted them immediately. If, as reported, they were just sitting around on the porch "loaded for bear," they could have presented a live theatre performance of "lying in wait." And of course there must have been an unserved outstanding warrant from when Tennessee Forestry firefighters met guns while attempting to stop a fire from spreading on Houston property.

The chain of family and associates could have kept them updated and alerted as the Kingston patrol moved toward Houston Hollow. Apparently there were official stops along the way that kept them in that area.

Then perhaps either Rocky or Leon, got an early word of the patrol car coming their way. Certainly one could have looked for the vehicle while the other already was concealed during that reported first pass. Practiced and ready, they would have had time to prepare for what was coming. After all, no one really knows "what is coming" unless they are the ones getting ready to let it loose. Those visiting friends would have softened the scene and enticed Jones and Brown to take a second look; in fact, to inquire about Rocky's whereabouts. Chilling.

Sound fact has it that anyone entering the area surrounding Houston Hollow was tracked for months before. A thinking person sees these people as either terribly bored or terribly quarrelsome. It did not add up to purpose-filled lives.

If these porch faces had nodded as if giving Jones the metaphorical time of day, it might have lowed Jones' risk assessment. For whatever reason they got him there. His long, long experience as a citizen and soldier failed him. And according to Gail Brown who had been the funeral director for the Houston family in April, "Billy Jones just wanted to be a hero." Apparently he ended up being just that.

Then again, the inevitability of such an encounter had publicized itself. The situation had crippled concord for years. Not being able to control the Houstons' boorish behavior had threatened the county's "domestic tranquility" while lying in wait much too long.

Not one person could explain when the Houston Doctrine replaced the rule of law, but agreed that to a good extent it had—at least in the vicinity of the family enclave. The deputy of the law breached Houston rule. According to the rule of law, Bill Jones had driven himself and his friend into their kill zone.

The law knew the dire circumstances that lay in a turbulent holding pattern. It was the law's job to get this home rule turned around. Leading up to the assault everyone but family members had been kept from using Barnard Narrows. No one forgot being turned around at gun point on the narrow road. No one who goes there can miss the darkness of the deeply-shadowed passage that gives off its own warnings. The western entrance to Houston Hollow is ominous. It could duplicate the secluded setting for early America's story of "Sleepy Hollow" and its headless horse man.

Indeed, the Houston brothers initiated a vitriolic trail of self-righteous arrogance against the entire constitutionally layered justice system. Weakened publicly with their years of gyrating promises to take out some cops, they may have hatched a plan to save face: By felling these two men, they cemented their boast. Perhaps in their minds, they realized their first victory——of sorts.

The resounding memories of Houston behavior stayed the same. Unashamedly, according to those close to them, "they were always on the look out for people they believed were out to get them." More privately held opinions concurred that the Houston brothers were no more than rough, mean "red necks."

Caught in their own trap and behind bars, they looked to that same criminal justice system they had condemned for decades to establish their innocence. Paying a serious price for their fanaticism was not in their program.

Rocky rambled and mouthed off as usual about bad lawyers and recusals. Of course he fired his defense attorney, sued him for millions, and later rehired him. All the while he looked meaner and got louder. In the end, he fired Attorney Rogers again; the judge stopped the sham and appointed Rogers as counsel. Both brothers appeared in one pretrial hearing after another, giving people a better look at bad.

Rocky was as cocky as ever. But his rhetoric became vapid. He never followed the well known anarchist Timothy McVeigh, who as one of the perpetrators in the bombing of the Oklahoma City Federal Building, strongly stood behind his own anti-government values until he died by lethal injection.

In the final analysis, the brothers were who they always had been. They were still the Houstons from Ten Mile, just south of Kingston and south of the Tennessee River. They wanted out on bond; had health care complaints; reportedly tried to break out of one jail; complained about their accommodations, and did get moved closer to home.

There was nothing new under the sun for these men and their ways.

Chapter 6

Man Hunt

Actually, the Houston Two's entire incredible con played out quite the same during the manhunt for them. Bombastic about their intentions, they did not hang around to shoot it out with insurmountable forces. That is the secret of their harassment propaganda. In that previous world of two against lone individual business owners and the like, their harassment tactics made them villainous bullies. Wearing that insidious body armor and toting guns even beyond Houston Hollow, they spread unmitigated fear. For sure, they always knew how to turn the claims against them inside out.

Satisfied that they had made their victims dead, the Houstons, as usual, ran to hide. Although missing, they wouldn't be for long!

Making a break for it required the help of Uncle Ray and Aunt Juanita (Houston Johnson). Speedily, with a hip and a hop, they rode their all terrain vehicle to the Johnson home about a ball field's distance away. Rocky had been shot in the hip. Of course an ambulance was out of the question, even though ambulances were on their way to the "officer down" call. Their blood lust made them wanted again.

That same Uncle Ray, who left the porch minutes before put them in his car. The Oak Ridge Medical Center they needed was a good 40 miles away. Not far into a back road escape, Rocky told Leon to get out and get going. He did. He left Roy's car at the Laurel Bluff Church of Christ cemetery, which is just across the road from large track of forested land owned by Bowater Paper Company (now AbitibiBowater). From there, he took off for the woods.

Perhaps the once again noted fugitives still were operating under their past illusions when they had made hide and seek a sport. Candidly a lot of people thought this might finally mean peace in the valley. This time they expected them to be down for the count.

Hundreds of law enforcement officers came streaming into Roane to help. The Federal Bureau of Investigation, the U.S. Marshal Service, Alcohol Tobacco and Firearms Agents, the Tennessee Bureau of Investigation, the Highway Patrol, and every police agency around—large and small—came out to bring them in. Flashing lights, men, dogs, helicopters, and those with the most recent technology met at Midway High School. The school had become the command center. This was Thursday, May 11th. Graduation ceremonies planned for Friday were cancelled.

Yet, with talk of Leon as a survivalist, he didn't reveal such unyielding behavior. Within a 24 hour period, Leon had turned himself in to the Tennessee Highway Patrol and Rocky was at the University of Tennessee Hospital recuperating. His wound required more than law enforcement first guessed it might.

Undoubtedly, Bill Jones and Mike Brown would have liked to have been given the same chances of survival and recovery.

Criminal behavior and criminal intent run deep according to the experts. Noted criminal sociologist Dr. Richard Rhodes, in his book *Why They Kill* professes that most who kill "make the decision to kill; it isn't suddenly upon them." For a fact, they had years and years to think about what they talked about doing.

In the end, Jones and Brown were targets of opportunity for them. That opportunity simply met desire. When it came to committing murder, they did not kill the powerful that they ranted on about. They kept the bar low and acted on their urge to "kill a few cops." Of course the two bad men did not attempt to kill The President of the United States, the United Sates Attorney General, or the Governor of Tennessee who, powerful and well-guarded, had always been beyond their reach. It could have been that in their minds, naming such names in their lawsuits felt good to them. Somehow documenting charges against those in the government's upper levels sent Rocky and Leon to believing their shared equal footing with the leadership of the United States. The fact is that their lawsuits documented Houston conspiracy theories that extended this far. At that point the riddle ended, but held out their angry babble in place.

Anxious to save their own hides, they were quick to kill the facts of their alleged homicides. What else? Rocky and Leon blamed Jones and Brown for initiating the one sided battle. That automatic rifle and banana clips attached carried the day. Conveniently the gun boosted illegal civilian fire power in the sense of a military AK-47, whether it was the Russian gun or copy of the original. Those first to arrive at the scene said the Houstons were the doers in a battle that lasted only seconds. This wasn't just cops talking. Today police are outgunned by criminals with such weapons. In view of the statistics large police forces and campus police are similarly arming their cops with the more lethal approach. Conclusively those on the scene concurred that the Ten Mile two also had put some thought into the homicides. They had made the decision to kill.

Apparently leaving no respect for the Houston name or ancestral home, the well-known brothers had stepped only a few paces from their bucolic Barnard Narrows porch to launch their bloody assault. Here in this valley, where the brothers Houston's antecedents had built the tall, imposing farmhouse about 70 years before, the "boys" had scorned the past. Successfully, these earlier Houstons remembered for their relocation from Union County, Tennessee to Roane become respected landowners and leaders there.

In the past the team Houston's contentions of conspiracy and harassment bought them public sympathy and attention. From May 11, 2006, the worst kind of notoriety would forever be attached to them: Even those who favored them would remember they had peppered their human targets with a barrage of penetrating bullets. They also had to admit that Rocky and Leon, acting on long-believed obsessions that pumped their adrenalin, had delivered two aberrant, baseless deaths with little risk to themselves. What was left to favor?

A favorable trial outcome would be all that could be salvaged here. Bringing justice to the newly dead meant everything. And once there, reasonable men and women would have to take a good look at the Houstons and their unquenchable hatred for those who governed.

Chapter 7

Homes within Range

Months prior to the deadly strike, another uncomfortable pattern led up to the deaths.

In hindsight, it looked as if the Houston pair were practiced and prepared for a show down. Ten Mile neighbors experienced what could best be described as "range practice," more commonly associated with routine law enforcement or military drills and training. Early evening gun shots resonated beyond the Houston properties to the hills and valleys surrounding them. The reported evening schedule, as gathered from individuals living within hearing range, left the neighbors edgy. Holding a population hostage is just that easy. Just who would be dumb enough to call in those suspicions to the sheriff's office? There were associated risks that their concerns could get back to the men. The more obvious objective went to the heart of the sound:

The alleged killers participated in a paramilitary style of range practice for a reason. Whether or not this behavior stemmed from their reported paranoia or their own sociopathic self-importance remains a bit murky. Maybe it was even their need to control and impress their followers. Evidence was rife for such speculation. According to neighbors, the recurring range activity sounded like preparation for war. Reports had it that those evening exercises occurred near 6 p.m., ultimately nearly paralleling the established time as the actual shootings. Folks capable of discriminating between gun shots fired confirmed what they believed to be the repetitious sounds of automatic and semi-automatic gunfire. Since the sounds coincided with routine farm chores, people outside on their own property noted a developing time line. As their local nightmare lay in wait, they squirmed with fright but remained reticent – a virtuous personal characteristic in East Tennessee.

The road into the hollow had been inhospitable for some time. Via the "grape vine," a few candid reports did made their way to law enforcement officials: That intelligence had come forward in bits and pieces about Rocky's and Leon's guiltless attitude as they commandeered the road. They apparently wanted to control more than their followers, which they made public here. There seemed to be more than enough talk about killing in Roane County. Without their outward display of grisly weapons, these puny looking men would not have been able to launch such a threat level. The encouragement of their groupies hastened that defiance of law and order.

Dressed as middle aged bandits, the Houston brothers were a formidable site. When two guys with semi-auto rifles (attached with extra rounds as reported) slung across their chests tell someone to turn around, he does. Too, it is unlikely he will return. With no one to stop them, the Houston behavior picked up. Even those bestowed with brawn gave into their own reasoning brains and did not confront them. Surreptitious word of mouth had it that not one person resisted. Who wanted to argue with the rifle clad men?

Although not an army artillery range, their property had been secured—and not by government but by fearsome individuals. In the length of time leading up to the gruesome end, as traffic had been cleared from that road, many wondered what lie in wait. Barnard Narrows, a public road, now was held by bandits.

Essentially, this was never meant to be an equal opportunity face off. Looking back, Rocky Houston had described the self-same killing zone when fleeing officers in 2005

Looking to pick Rocky Joe up on an outstanding warrant then, city officers found him at Kingston's United States Post Office. But he bolted. Although miles home to that privatized valley of hundreds of acres, he appeared dead set on getting there. Officers always feared what to expect. Quickly, the alerted city patrol fell in behind the county patrol as Rocky fled the town's jurisdiction into the county. There the county patrol led the Highway 58 chase south, followed by additional city officers.

Rocky's 2005 run looked different this time: he overturned his pick-up during the police pursuit. Every law abiding person knows to pull over when flashing lights tail you. Most people do just that. The law knew him well and wanted to bring him in without violence. Following professional procedure the deputies, in order to stop him, threw out spikes in front of his pickup truck. They then blocked his car, ending the chase without civilian injuries in oncoming traffic.

The younger Houston offered no surprise to bystanders when he passed forward his usual lame excuse: He said he ran because he had no plans to stop until he got home where he could trust people. In his best and last plan, home was going to be more than a place of the heart.

Having gone not quite far enough to reach the hollow of the clannish Houston family, the law cut him off before he got to his destination. And then and there, those same people that he couldn't trust, those same people who were out to kill him and his family, watched with drawn guns as he crawled from his pickup truck with his gun pointed at them.

They could have shot him. They didn't.

So, as friends of the brothers thundered complaints forward against Rocky's mistreatment on the highway, he and those who were kin, or had an emotional kinship with him, overlooked the considerations and patience of law enforcement. As usual someone else was to blame. And those grandstanding Rocky's and Leon's moves were more convinced than every their favorites were harassment victims. The terrible two, touting themselves as harassed, continued to be their own best publicists. Professional publicists couldn't have done better. In Rocky Joe's case, home had long been considered more than heart felt.

Wiley Rocky, for years had kept his family community in mind as home base on game day. Once he hit the imaginary home plate, no one successfully could call him out. If they did, he was counting on family support. True? By now it was clear that regardless of circumstances, family ties here meant that a portion of the Houston crowd was willing to circle its wagons against the outside world. It meant none of the large family clan would hear or speak or see evil against their family. Comments following the deaths included, "I can't say anything, I am related to them." And this is America. With liberty and justice for all?

In hindsight, that safe haven Rocky Houston referred to in January of 2005 clearly resonates as the place that had taken shape as his militarized zone. Right there on that public road, the two had staked out their patch of turf. With legality out of the question, the Houston clan privatized a public road and eliminated the public right of passage.

Predictably, plans would be laid to pick them up on their warrants. Predicting that fact, they must have begun sweeping the road of outside vehicles weeks before the ambush. That sweep looks to have eliminated the possibility of outside witnesses.

Also predictable were Rocky's taunts of law enforcement. He knew how to look like a victim. Looking to make himself a martyr in his Harriman courtroom speeding citation he yelled at court officers to "cuff" him—"I know the routine." His own routines and that of authorities waited to tango, in a sense Rocky and Leon Houston cleverly had orchestrated a full dance recital.

Those well-developed antics got up close and personal when Tennessee Governor Phil Bredesen countered them in a state SWAT team. The governor authorized a joint SWAT operation in 2003 with Rocky's name on it. He had pushed his threats to the limit. Somehow, HE got credit for coming out of his home on that warrant at the behest of his preacher. The truth is that that SWAT operation was authorized to use deadly force if he didn't. Approving the preacher's first entry to "talk him out" was standard procedure. However successful the plan was then, the experienced bad man had just learned more. He picked up on another "routine" here and must have believed he had perfected it.

He must have conceived a plan then and there that would eliminate his disadvantage in another SWAT operation. Few would doubt his criminal versatility or his mind set. In fact both brothers' need to control was written all over their long term behavior. Authority, any authority, was their enemy.

Doing the arithmetic adds up: The Houston twosome most definitely went on to segregate access to the area for any SWAT teams which might return. No SWAT could conceal itself in a delivery van or other covert vehicle while they were in control. But the stress of the waiting game must have gnawed at them. Although it would have been by far smarter and simpler to have turned themselves in on the outstanding warrant, they didn't.

Still, as often repeated by hundreds of similar law breakers, they probably itched for a stand off; but they would choose one that ultimately would favor them. These men thrived on the stimulation of daring acts, even if such inspiration would lead up to the grand finale.

Getting the jump on those "cops" would prop up their "brags" and bogus bravery. No doubt an assessment of their manhood came into play. Selling themselves on their combative, anti-government hero characterization was as essential as selling it to others.

Indeed, there were those who felt law enforcement should stay out of Houston Territory. That concept, which many became to recite as somewhat of a truism, was preposterous and weak. The last time anyone asked, America was still a free country; and, whether it was the Houstons or big city gangs, no one owned the neighborhood. Law enforcement officers with legally issued but lesser weapons took huge risks. No one else would have wanted to or would have been asked to take back an illegally secured road. In light of that scenario, Jones and Brown were heroes. They gave their lives in a battle. No other good citizen soldiers had to die at the hand of the Houstons.

But on that one fatal Thursday evening in May 2006, according to early after-action crime scene reports, the men with powerful weapons and a feint or two won the battle. And the sun set on the brothers' side of the mountain.

Chapter 8

Grew Fat on Kindness

Many locals believe "Sheriff Haggard grew fat on kindness." A close look at the Houston brothers' past fifteen years might portray their enemy Sheriff David Haggard as somewhat of a humanitarian, if not a saint. During that period, he seems to have characterized a number of the Houstons' acts as mere shenanigans.

Contrary to these less than ominous revelations, Rocky and Leon saw Sheriff Haggard as their number one enemy. How wrong the duo seems to have been.

Evidence provided by numbers of law enforcement officers establishes a deepening divide as to the Houstons' maliciousness and how that behavior endangered the public welfare. Small groups of citizens and law enforcement saw the now evolving public personalities and their threats as serious. The same group thought Haggard had coddled the growth of the terrible two's menacing activity. But a few close to the sheriff, according to other voices, agreed with their boss's evaluation of the men.

Then again by 2000, more and more county officers had formed a consensus that Haggard did not support them as professions on this issue, and, in fact, had taken a paternalistic direction with his treatment of the Houstons.

But Haggard knew these Houstons and family members. With 39 years in law enforcement to include twelve years as Roane County Sheriff, he was experienced and good at what he did. Part of this time he was chief deputy under his predecessor Sheriff Arnold Clower. Indeed, he knew them too well to overlook the potential of Leon's and Rocky's escalating and threatening behavior.

However, for the most part, the seasoned sheriff seemed to let it fly. Privately, he must have carried some concerns about the two-of-a-kind brothers to work. Outwardly, he maintained somewhat of a live-and-let-live position with them. He balanced his humanitarian nature with a different nature: the nature of criminals.

Dissimilarly, the brothers saw none of Haggard's interpreted kindness and patience. To them he was a foe to be conquered. After all, Rocky sued him at least twice in federal court, albeit unsuccessfully. The claims carried no facts. A lay person might describe them as rambling flights of fancy—hardly the material of collected minds.

The court's decision, after sorting through the complaints and answers required, never accepted the empty muddled claims. The succinct diction of these knowledgeable answers and appraisals left nothing with which to go forward. The Houstons' ideas never touched on fact. But erudite explanations just did not matter to the brothers: for them the court's response stood as a temporary obstacle. Nothing deterred them from filing more self-styled law suits. The whirling dervishes just went back with repetitive law suits. One of the Houstons' inane lawsuits against the Sheriff Haggard preceded the homicides, and one followed it. Their narrow vision focused on Haggard; and, with men like them, narrow was what drove them to their crimes.

The Houston family and friends stood behind their belief that the county lawman continued to persecute the tight brothers. If asked, as always, those followers let out a flood water of anger that eclipsed known facts. This loyalty seemed to be based on the Houstons' control over others. Without that parade of supporters, they probably would have been overlooked and forgotten.

Piling on their usual victims—the Sheriff and his officers—was popular as usual. And as usual, this talk helped clear the way for Rocky and Leon to move about with unending accusations against authority figures generally, but particularly the Sheriff. Strangely, this part of the community dedicated to the two, indulgently romanticized that radical behavior like late 1960's groupies. For certain, emotions surrounding the dangerous men always went way off psychological charts.

Actually, it was Jack Stockton who stood as a rampart against Houston's continuing bad acts. First as a police officer and then as Harriman's top cop, Stockton long had had professional difficulty with the South of the River at Ten Mile natives when they frequented his Harriman town limits. Stockton believed for years that the Houstons' fanatic, out-of-control behavior would certainly become deadly. He stood strong against what he feared.

Sheriff Haggard did not agree or verbalize such deadly fears until after the fact. Then he spoke about his warnings. He said that he alerted his deputies for weeks to stay clear of the Houston compound following the death of their mother, sixty-six year old Juanita Carol Houston, who died Easter week 2006. Her family buried her Easter Sunday in the family plot behind her home on Barnard Narrows. Again, he seemed the humanitarian. And he knew more:

Sheriff Haggard saw their mother as the authority figure that, on occasion, the men had looked to for censure. Now gone, he believed anything was possible. Again he understood and even predicted an accelerated loss of emotional restraint from the men. Perhaps the logic was strong, but the timing was wrong. The sage he appears to have been should have shared his down-home perspective on motherhood and sons much earlier. A mother's balance in problem solving can mean everything.

However among a number of deputies and the community itself, Haggard was said to have lost respect over the years. A Roane County Courthouse parking lot murder and escape would also support the attitudes. Here he didn't have the foresight he seemed to exhibit with the Houston family. It seemed he was standing in line waiting to make the next bad step. And the Houstons were waiting for him to make it. The perception seemed to be that lawlessness had an edge. Then came the death of Deputy Jones and Mike Brown.

Failures add up here for Haggard. His slow, old-school decisions look terribly wrong. Perhaps, his long term tactics were too long term. Perhaps in hindsight he had refused to adjust his historic perceptions to the present. And perhaps he lingered during his last years of tenure, falling down on the job because his was an old timer. Reaching back to his earlier experience didn't seem to work anymore. In other words, the way he dealt with criminals "once upon a time" would no longer seize the day; nor would it stop the bad guys.

Roane County had grown, and the need to stay ahead of the burgeoning crime that had grown with it meant everything. Although David Haggard, good guy, had speculated that without a mother's wisdom circumstances could go from bad to worse quickly, he had all ready treaded water much too long. According to plenty of comment, he had not stayed up to speed.

To understand "old school" perceptions, one needed to go back nearly forty years earlier. About that time David Haggard began earning his way in law enforcement.

"In the day," moonshine held its own as a source of viable income. And whether you purchased "white lightning" from the man who made it or the law, the decision was only a matter of preference.

Of course any sheriff then went through the business of rounding up stills. That was his job. Publicly displaying such booty authenticated a job well done. And that custom in Roane County took place in front of the painfully old, small county jail. The apparatus used to distill the "hard liquor" didn't say much for itself, but it did speak well for the sheriff's successful moonshine raids. Once done in defiance of the "Feds," local mountain men knew how to make hard liquor. The balance between those who made it and those expected to confiscate it could be precarious. Perhaps there had been a bit of conspiracy then and there.

But, as a historic fact, almost every sheriff took some of the best confiscated alcohol for himself and some for friends. That behavior mixed with the prevalent Baptist religion throughout the South, lent itself to the saying that most states (and counties) "voted dry and drank wet." Easy enough to decipher: Those who made the "shine" stayed in business by supporting the churches that were against it. Very slowly legal liquor made its way to Roane County. By 2006 there were a couple liquor stores right near the court house. One is ironically named "Bootleggers." Of course marijuana, crack cocaine, Ecstasy and any number of designer drugs took over the roadhouse scene. But, no one in Roane County would honestly believe that the old school's devil moonshine has completely vanished.

The Roane County law worked differently then. They seldom served warrants on relatives, or anyone they knew or liked. Those warrants would just languish or disappear. But when those same deputies brought a habitual agitator into jail they served justice personally: Once taken into custody, these trouble makers, according to living witnesses, were hit with black jacks, brass knuckles, and solid punches by arresting officers. Tried and true back then, this seems to have deterred a few "wan'a bes" from developing higher criminal profiles. That was the way. That was the day.

With the honky tonks of country music lyrics scattered up and down U.S. Highway 70, there was plenty of nightlife and fighting from Roane's Eastern Standard Time right on to and over Rockwood Mountain and the Central Time Zone. The great equalizer then was the "Saturday Night Special"—a gun carried to hold up your side of a "mix it up" in such places. The typical weapon was usually considered a piece of junk, but available at a low price. Saturday entertainment there always included your own or someone else's alcohol, and most always meant mean drunks or just mean people. Old timers remember the protocol: If someone offered you a drink and you turned him down, he would put a gun to your head and change your decision on the spot. If you didn't oblige the request, the possibility of dead on the bar room floor was real. And of course there were a lot of "shoot 'em ups" in these places. No different in some ways was the fact that if you had a good lawyer you eventually were free with a coveted reputation. Free, and feared now by many, no one would mess around with you.

The Houston brothers were born to the life. And their South of the River community could hold their own against anyone. Apparently the culture survives some there.

"Old school" humanitarian aid was also built into the sheriff's social service efforts. When a derelict needed food, deputies put the abandoned man in jail to clean him up and feed him for awhile. The town drunk could get the same weekend consideration, with a bit of old time religion added to clear out his head. A volunteer preacher would lift him up a bit before he was turned out of jail.

Understanding and small talk helped a bit too. Seldom was a person truly homeless in the sense of being closed-out by family. "Taking care of your own" was a principle to live by in Roane County. On the other hand, no uproar was made if a citizen took up a BB gun to pop a repeat offender and rid him from squatting on his property. The law worked at keeping it simple.

Today there is nothing simple about maintaining the peace anywhere. Today criminals, crime syndicates, and gangs outnumber the cops. Sometimes the "bad boys" (and girls) go farther: They wear bullet proof vests, have access to bigger and more deadly guns than most law enforcement carries, and secure financial means for enabling and disabling technology. Least to deny is the plethora of criminal activity over the internet. Policing has steadily become more dangerous and more sophisticated.

For that matter, riding along with a patrolling officer has become so dangerous that it has become passé. Police departments interviewed said that their insurance carriers no longer allow the once customary policy of "ride-alongs." Jim Washam, Kingston's top cop, says that only reserve officers can ride along.

Things change fast. Nothing stays the same. Squires no longer take part in Roane County government as they once did. The Anglophile term of "High Sheriff" has found a haven in history, and Roane County constables are working to hold on to their positions.

In the same vein, the brothers Houston no longer can fantasize inheriting a family fiefdom or "old school" culture. And ex-Sheriff Haggard has learned that, unlike Merlin in King Arthur's Court, he failed as a wizard.

Chapter 9

Stockton's New School

Indeed, the then soon to be elected Roane Sheriff Jack Stockton, midway through 2006, replaced the "old school" David Haggard. Stockton had a knack for law enforcement, a part of which he credited to his early association with William Birl Jones. Jones had been his training officer then.

The county officer who the Houstons killed had taught him a lot of about hard core police work. Jones had come into law enforcement by way of Marine Sergeant and United States Army Ranger. He had been a cop for 25 years.

In Harriman as a young officer, Stockton saw Jones as a man who believed in his mission: He went after bad guys. Just knowing him was an inspiration to fight crime. Much of that same Jones' agenda has stayed with Sheriff Stockton throughout his own career. Reminiscing about the relationship, Stockton said Bill was a "cop's cop, a man who wouldn't back down in fear." Today, Jack Stockton is just as determined to take a bite out of crime as was Deputy Jones, the man who died doing it.

Stockton, perhaps predictably, became Harriman's Police Chief; and after the death of Jones, Roane County elected him Sheriff. Unfalteringly, he has fought crime. His professional alliance with Kingston Police Chief Jim Washam has been valuable to both. Washam, a big man of few words, has had the Hoss Cartright character seen in TV's 1970's Bonanza since he was a kid growing up in the county schools and graduating from Roane County High

School. He stood tall quietly then and does now. Whenever he speaks he has something meaningful to say. Almost inimitably, he listens and learns.

So it is that the two adept men agree on how to approach crime from the outside in: They both understand crime's nuances and observe them closely. They look hard at fact, yet acknowledge the scope of criminal fantasies and the relevant statistics that can, and do, result in realities.

According to Washam, Jack Stockton never isolates his fears or his conjecture. With the Houstons, he positioned his actions like a weather vane, seeking to undermine incriminating crime clouds on the horizon. But Stockton did not keep this knowledge hidden. Instead, he worried where the Houston path might go and shared his theories among responding law enforcement. All area chiefs, to include Kingston, Harriman, Rockwood, Oliver Springs, and Oak Ridge, wanted solutions.

As the group met and conferred, their insights targeted the Houston's accelerating extreme behavior. The top cops developed a "to do" list to keep law enforcement alert to the all deadly possibilities. Of course the Houstons had to be high on the list. They definitely attracted their own attention.

Now anyone going into Houston territory to make an arrest for years expected violence. And the crimes fell right in with local crime prognosticators' forecasts. After the deaths, the general public could better measure the need to carry out the law.

The joint task force of city and county officers successfully visited Barnard Narrows following the May shootings to bring in a Houston cohort in July on his own warrant. Washam says previously Haggard had been slow to act.

Without a hitch or bullet fired the joint county force successfully transported the Houston associate back to the jail. And on that occasion, they set up a professionally-driven SWAT operation. The only one surprised was the young man. The plan to net him culminated from complaints about his chorused threats to kill both a Kingston father and his daughter. The alarmed man had had consistent threats that had kept his family in fear. The father complained to the locals and back to Haggard until there was agreement on the jointly planned effort.

From the outside, a tipster told local police that the friend of the Houstons was seen hiding out in the Houston compound. With additional pressure from the frightened family, Haggard agreed to the plan to pick up the accused. With the best know strategies in place, a normal looking service vehicle went into the valley like a Trojan horse loaded with law enforcement. The element of surprise and excellent planning brought the subject in to face his charges.

The necessity for alarm in this case went against the Houston crowd's idea of justice. But it worked. The community seems to have gone too long allowing them their way. No matter how wrong, the clan and their ilk always complained of being badgered by the law. And regardless of their attempts to upend simple justice, their behavior drew a continuing crowd. Plenty wanted "a dog in the fight" against the law.

When posters went up in the Courthouse portraying the possibilities of upcoming violent Houston conduct, Rocky and Leon voiced their indignation within the ramblings of one of their often filed lawsuits. Oh my, even though their spreading insurgency had its roots right there in the courthouse, they felt violated. They felt they could twist things around like obdurate school children. Their venomous attitudes were backed up by venomous lawsuits against multiple individuals in the courthouse workforce. Employees who alerted each other with posters to possible lockdown situations knew what there was to be afraid of. National crime data, in fact shows that targeted courthouse employees have been injured and killed by similar other anti-government hot heads. They had hard reasons to post their alarm.

So it was that many people wanted the Houstons to be stopped: No one wanted to be their victims. Holding the governing part of the community in wait of things to come seemed to have worked in the bold brothers' favor. When ever men can roam a justice center pushing their intended wave of hatred against numerous individuals there, something has already gone too far. Just normal good thinking would stand behind any specific voiced or printed warnings. Better, of course would be putting a stop to them. In fact, negative as it was, Jones's and Brown's deaths brought about Rocky's and Leon's capture and pre-trail imprisonment. Their alleged felony murders still lay in wait while they made spectacles of themselves as usual. The government they hated gave them access to every opportunity. That is what America is all about.

In retrospect, Harriman's Chief Stockton and his brotherhood of close municipal chiefs (Rockwood's Bill Stinnett and Kington's Jim Washam) shared a crime calendar. Those farther away in Oliver Springs and Oak Ridge were right there to help whenever they could. They all wanted to cooperate in tightening up their own war against threatening crime in Roane County. Sharing their Houston insights steeled them for the turbulent, ongoing Houstons—who issued threats both subtle and not so subtle— which they so much wanted to bring to a conclusion.

But bringing terminal conclusions to the brotherhood's ungovernable behavior or that of their associates just could not go forward without the Roane County Sheriff's sanction. Reportedly, he refused to understand the other chiefs' perceived angst: "I just don't believe those boys are going to hurt anybody." The Roane Sheriff either lost sight of his obligation or lost the will to deal with them any longer. After all, from the time Leon had been picked up on a gun charge it had been close to twenty years. Their emboldened behavior remained static over the years to follow.

And so, those few good men kept a vigilant watch since they could not convince Haggard, the country's larger law enforcement figure, to lead them in a consolidation of action directed at the community's protection. But they did keep watch and discuss possibilities as they waited for the sheriff to act in his countywide capacity. In the end it took a seasoned warrior and the accord of those above him to defeat the Houston anarchy. Their esprit de corps finally worked to stop incurable, unstable bullies—bent on anarchy. In hindsight, the price was steep. It is too bad that the dead men could not stand up to them in death as they had in life so that their own audience could applaud.

Chapter 10

Heritage Stands Up

Roane County inherited a bent toward brave hearts not bullies. The citizens of the county named after Archibald Roane, Tennessee's second governor, are guarded geographically to their east by the primitive mountains of the Southern Appalachian mountain range. Although rather heterogeneous now, many of those early settlers were Scotch and Irish descendants, or Scots-Irish. They chose the terrain that to some extent reminded them of the homeland they had left behind when coming to America. Still today, they are known for their fighting and moral courage. Among them live many "Brave Heart[s]," as in the Mel Gibson film of that name. They are clannish, independent, and familiar with Sir William Wallace, the Scottish patriot who stood for justice, while living and dying with a brave heart. James Webb, nationally known author and United States Senator from Virginia refers to these American counterparts in his book *Why We Fight*.

No one would debate Appalachia's reputation. The recognized mountaineer heritage occasionally has carried with it feuding, fighting, and killin'. But the rumored ambush and assault that ended the lives of the deputy and his ride-along buddy—himself a young stroke victim—defied that Scots-Irish code of honor and justice: It was not just the unwarranted killing, but the merciless intent identified with their staged choice of unevenly matched weapons.

Once in America, before dueling was outlawed, political rifts could spark a duel. Most often "seconds" stood in for each side to mediate an apology.

But, if the event went forward, each side agreed to place, time, and weapons. History looks back badly on barbarian show downs which had even been codified. Yet, if this approach to political disagreement was ever meant to be chivalrous, the Houstons sidestepped the mannerly part. They also seemed to have coveted every opportunity to hide and wait for their opportunities to win at crime.

So along with brave versus cowardly theories in Roane County, people wanted fair fights. This was a brave kind of place where more Tennesseans fought for America's causes than those from any other state. In the Houstons' case, there would be no debate about their documented running home to hide. The law looks at hiding oneself for the purpose of committing a crime as lying in wait. When it comes down to murder it defines it as "malice aforethought," or just plain murder.

Heritage looks harshly on the magnitude of the deadly results. Disgrace is cast on those who commit aberrant blood thirst. That blatant need to destroy could not be concealed. The killers' momentary assault shredded the men's bodies. Caught off guard and unable to drive on or get out of their patrol car, they died trapped within. For all appearances, the crime scene pointed to what cities know as a "drive by shooting." But this "drive by" was reversed.

In the Houston brothers' years of personally prefigured wide spread conspiracy against them, their self-filed lawsuits always asked for high dollar damages. They believed those combined claims should far exceed the millions and millions of various state lottery winners. So, in fact they sought their own rewards for their expressed pain and suffering but gave no consideration to handing down the pain and suffering they put on Jones and Brown. A history of moral empathy or self-reproach was not part of the Houston doctrine.

And then there were the Commandments, the ten that we all know. The devout Christians of East Tennessee look harshly at violating those rules. A good Christian knows that murder is not an option. Nearly every home has a Bible that lifts and directs families in such troubled times. But this barefaced sin stretched the mind's forgiveness level. They talked among themselves about how sinfully defiant a man must be to electrify the flesh of his victims with such overkill. The license taken went far beyond the Sixth Commandment of "Thou Shall Not Kill" to multiply that damage.

So, what can't a good Christian man understand? Unless, of course, it might be calculated differently by someone who satisfies his twisted motives with the likes of this unusual killing. Dead by death trap emerged as the objective. It would take a jury to decide. Of course, everyone knows that dead men tell no tales. The circumstances and justice served would now depend on the dynamics of the living.

To be argued was the defense table's suggestion that the Houston two took defensive positions behind trees or elsewhere to save themselves from the county patrol's attempt to kill them. Of course the defense is allowed to throw out almost any idea that might move a jury to find a reasonable doubt in the prosecution's effort to convict. Of course the prosecution held to murder charges that meant the "boys" had been "lying in wait" to take out the men in the car.

Offensive positions behind trees or hills or buildings are more often sought and recognized. Setting up offensive action is planned. The link between the time and the opportunity to hide is even clear to kids playing hide and seek. The one seeking is at a disadvantage. Here the Houstons, hiding, clearly could see the marked car moving into view and approaching. Jones and Brown would have had no warning and could only have reacted to their final circumstances when faced with the brothers Houston and their guns.

In a required trial defense of their actions the gruesome twosome built on untruths as quickly as they could bring them forth in their motion hearings which was to lead up to an eventual trial.

Yes, they deceptively had vilified government for years. In lawsuits they named big names far from their physical reach: national figures who had never heard of them and who would not respond to their ridiculous subpoenas. They also dipped down to clerks and low level officials, making each spend money to seek attorney representation. But now it was Bill Jones and Mike Brown whom they claimed they were defending themselves against; and Jones and Brown had never once in the bold brothers' lawsuits been mentioned as conspirators or warring parties. Now they wanted their audience to believe that the two dead men also had been part of the grand conspiracy against them. In a way, nothing really changed. The brothers Houston were just a bunch of twist and shout! Part of that twist went even to their decision to be represented by lawyers—their most hated profession. In due course that wouldn't work either. For Rocky and Leon it was always blame, blame and shame, shame.

Chapter 11

Weapons Win

Back on May 11, 2006, the Houstons had the responsibility to retreat into their home. Getting the jump in order to protect the road or the yard didn't exist. The small group once on the porch retreated or dispersed early when told there would be trouble. They ran fast enough to diagnosis the severity of that kind of trouble. Who wouldn't if they had eaten a companionable lunch with high powered assault weapons?

Now look who stayed: The terrible two who could have and should have gone into the house just feet away. And yes, within their home the guns might have given them more liberty with the law. It didn't happen that way. Criminals do not abide by the law. The cops have to go after them. Some question where that last soldier will come from. As the temperatures rise fewer and fewer sign up for the job. Without them, innocents will find no civilized, safe harbor.

In this case, and according to initial testimony, the women who ran from the porch were also the women who sounded the alarm. Much like sentries, the friends called out that the patrol car was turning back for a second pass by the old Houston homestead. Uncle Ray Johnson says he left the porch at this point upon Leon's request. According to early reports the women in anticipation of the deadly encounter sprinted from the scene. They became defense witnesses as expected. But one must wonder who truly the witnesses to the alleged murders were. There were no cameras there. Right?

Jumping to "defensive" positions, out beyond the porch, Rocky and Leon must have been ready and waiting. Their offensive postures are hard to deny. And premeditation is hard to miss. Only moments of decision are required to prove premeditation. Legal minds know that such consideration is "for a length of time, no matter how short." Reflection on their long term hype throughout the community "to kill some cops" seals the probability of planned intent.

The chaste porch picnic of "Vienna sausage and chocolate milk" also stood as a defense more than two years later in probable cause hearings. Their lawyer, no doubt intending to soften the crime and the rough exterior of heartless men, gave the initial crime scene a mellow brush stroke.

Imagine. There the anti-government men sat propped up on the porch intending to enjoy a mellow early evening with their semi and automatic weapon sidekicks beside them. The weight of these weapons must have contributed as much stomach acid as the food. What were they waiting for anyway? A guess might suggest adrenalin ruled and held them in place. At least in Rocky's case. Anyone who knew him said he lived nervously on the edge of things. Leon was as devoted to Rocky as a brother could be. Both were evidently rock hard in mind and spirit.

Later, recanted testimony from the porch "lookouts" came as no surprise. The group was as tight knit as a legion of soldiers. The weapons they preferred, according to those familiar with their lifestyles, were designed, or copied, from those used for war. This Houston war, which lasted nearly two decades, had continued longer than any war in United States history.

Everyone on the porch knew what was coming. The commanders had given orders: They designed a hot zone and knew no one else wanted to stay. Logic says they all somehow participated in what was coming down the pike. Yet, looking closely, not one of those on the porch with the brothers themselves would have carried out such a heinous act. Perhaps the terrible two had backed into an act of "show and tell." They had told it for so long that they needed to do more that talk to keep the devoted believing in them. The brothers were armed and ready to give those returning cops more than they could survive. Perhaps, as a few speculated, those bullet proof vests they were known to sport would have fit the occasion.

The men in the car were not so equipped. No bullet proof vests, no assault rifles, and no place to hide. And who wouldn't have donned body armor if they were going to start a shooting match with the Barnard Narrows men? Actually, the report that Jones had put a shotgun into his trunk that evening was enough to encourage the accused men's supporters in their defense. While carrying along a shotgun is a common practice among law enforcement professions, locals don't seem to understand the rules. Anyway, it was reportedly in the trunk and wouldn't have been useful under the circumstances. No shotgun would be useful against the alleged assault rifles of the Houstons. And again, what use is it in the truck of your vehicle?

The Houston assault weapon(s), or similar knockoff assault rifles, or real military rifles can have a clip which holds 30 (and sometimes as many 100) high velocity bullets. In this case, banana clips expanded the bullet's limit. The speed of those bullets alone can pass straight through a man. Undeniably, Leon seemed to have had a semi-automatic pistol and not the assault weapon reported over the earlier months. Still, isolated and somewhat unaware of the nation's modernity and need to maintain lawfulness, the large community south of the Tennessee River had voiced the unfairness of road spikes used against the Houstons. No one on their side felt the multiple accelerated rifle rounds with clips attached were unfair.

As crime across the country mounts, germane knowledge about cops who are out-gunned and unprotected is rife. Nowadays newsworthy criminals carry automatic rifles, wear body armor, and have all the technology out there. Then too, few armed officers carry the fire power those two sent out. Here and there that is changing. Some federal and local police are equipped to meet the challenge of the guns that saturate Third World Countries.

As part of the county's third shift that evening, Jones left his home to patrol a disappearing patch of nature's best terrain. His job required him as a representative of county government to protect and serve the Roane citizens who believed in the rule of law versus outright mayhem. Mike Brown was just out attempting to make his life a bit better by being with his friend on this fateful evening.

Apparently, Rocky and Leon shot the two because they caught them off guard. Choosing the time and place made their deadly game so easy. Choosing to make their arguments personal by killing the men they hardly knew came as a surprise. Their wide net of random "crazy" behavior must have worked hard on their lives.

What was coming out of their dark vision was only something they knew. There it was like a sprung leak in a damn. They never had shown the discipline required to take a different path. They were dead set on destruction. Dark clouds held them in place. And with that dead end stance, their revolution ended as well.

Chapter 12

Resolution to Revolution

Little doubt exists that lawlessness prevails where government fails. In the end government scores its own failures and successes at the polls and in court. Civilization's rule of law conceptualizes itself as a balanced scale, as in the scales of justice motif. And, positively in this case, humble citizens ruled and balanced the law's past with a potential for the future: Enough of mayhem in Roane County.

By the end of the day on May 11, the County had had its fill of drama and of what was perceived as bad government. Deputy Jones' and his comrade Mike Brown's sudden and merciless deaths marked the end of inconclusive decisions.

Both the courts and law officers seemed to have twiddled their thumbs through indecision and intimidation. Each was trying hard to be fair minded. And with this, their authority seemed to dissipate.

Perhaps their humanitarian decision making had been extended beyond the pale. That is a hard one to call. Sadly, but finally, the men's deaths ended it.

According to a minority of persons talking openly before the trail (and they were a sparse few), the two men's deaths were preventable. And that opinion came from those who opposed the Houstons as well as those who supported them. Speaking like a sage, Clarence Robbins, respected old timer and twenty-year chief investigator for the Roane Sheriff's department, saw Jones' and Brown's deaths as a "preventable tragedy."

While some citizens shook their heads over the outcome of the anti-government pair who was quickly charged with felony murder, others prepared to change things. With county elections just months away, people joined to speak their minds with silent but decisive votes: So it was that on August 3, 2006 the standing Sheriff David Haggard, long tenured District Attorney General Scott McCluen, and much of his office staff, lost their jobs. In the simplest terms, Roane citizens fired them. More specifically they routed them with losses two to one in favor of their opponents. But blame is easier to cast then change.

Perhaps the horrific country style execution also condemned the community at large. For a time the alleged killers cast more weight than the good judgment of reasonable others. Attempting to bridle the miscreants had never slowed the Houstons violent ambitions. So the community itself fell to lying in wait. This long wait continued to hover like a looming cloud, even as a projected July 14, 2008 trial date approached.

Actually, the area South of the River recently had seen a man "sent up" for shooting at Tennessee officials clearing marijuana growth; another man killed a neighbor in the man's front yard; and then that convict's girlfriend who helped him escape by killing his guard in the courthouse parking lot. To beat it all, a federal task force brought in high profile Atlanta drug dealer who had been living in Ten Mile when he worked his multi-million dollar Knoxville connection. Yes: Right there in Ten Mile, often known as Houston territory.

When the community got its equilibrium, it stood up. This was the U.S.A., not Baghdad. Democracy took hold and brought back healthy government. Not surprisingly, the Houstons must have overlooked this possible change in attitude. But then, no one ever said the Houston guys stayed awake during their public school civics classes. However, the mean team of Rocky and Leon for much too long had successfully shared a quarrelsome and reactionary strategy to boot the law.

Digging deep, there may have been a private and deeply held nexus of anger in their early lives. Some people made very subtle undefined references to the possibility. But that is where the study of crime and criminals can quickly overlook the victims. Excuses, excuses.

If long term personal rejection or depression escalated into this act of unforgivable outrage, their psychological workups never pointed to origins of bad childhoods or hidden cruelty. And there, almost all criminals are as willing to pass the guilt as they are to pass the chicken and dumplin's in Ten Mile.

Certainly something long-term stoked the boys' to men's criminal intent. Self-disciplined boundaries keep a lot of folks straight. Willful behavior has no boundaries. And the only boundaries the Houstons drew were for others—as in this is the United States of Houston down "har," on Barnard Narrows Road, "South of the River," Ten Mile, Tennessee.

Clearly, the Houston revolution was more often a degree of tantrums and territorial mindsets than it was a "sovereign citizen's" revolution. Those similar groups also depended on paper terrorism harassment, short wave and internet communication, frivolous lawsuits, vigilante courts, fictitious automobile lawsuits and schools of common law. As a loosely tied union of anti-government groups, the radical faction had even declared a "Republic of Texas."

The men's local extremists' code of conduct could have emerged from a range of sought marks on a map of other anti-government groups such as the Montana Freeman. A source conversant with the brothers said Rocky had talked about giving up his United States citizenship. Without definitive details to add to this sort of inspiration, there seems little doubt that they would have reached for some inclusion in the once popularized thinking. In reality they were left out on a limb. Many of the 90's extremists had abandoned their fanaticism or gone underground. Neurotically the Houtstons went ahead and tested that limb.

The brothers Houston's rant and rave rather caused them to be overlooked a bit. The inefficiency of the high strung brothers' apparent philosophy really never developed into deeper possibilities to observers. And while similar set values went public across the nation in the 90's, the Ten Mile revolution for minimalist government was left alone. Rocky's and Leon's aberrant behavior eclipsed what could have been the heart of the matter. Had this connection been physically uncovered, the federal government would have gone after them as those "domestic terrorists" they themselves had called others.

For them, living within the laws of the larger community beyond Houston territory was out of the question. The men stuck to their agitating agendas. Prideful outsiders that they were, they did not seek any good faith intent to reconcile their problems with others. The Houston two just wanted to set everyone straight. They were territorial people. They were intolerant and inflexible as well. Without the education or the emotional intelligence to realize the trouble that awaited them, they kept pushing forward like angered bulls. No country gentlemen, they lived divisive lives.

The Houston two continued their repeated conduct anyway. They suffered surreal lives, perhaps maintaining some self-respect that was otherwise missing. From an observer's point of view, their unrelenting fanciful lawsuits nourished the need to be acknowledged—albeit in the worst way.

Once without any standing in the community, they had purchased some. Being renegades with a reputation brought acknowledgement they must never have dreamed possible. Characteristically known to crime experts, that same recognition encouraged them to frighten, flee, fight, file false allegations, and allegedly commit felony murder.

Before the multiple small town jurisdictions and sheriff's department could commit on joint decision making, the aging 45-year-old Rocky Joe and 47-year-old Clifford Leon had done their dirty deed. Behind bars, the co-dependents bellowed as usual. But, as alleged killers, their behavior was commonplace. Jailed, they seemed to find solid fraternity of thought. Like others in prison garb, they continued to whine about accommodations, bad lawyers (sued the one for $7 million and then rehired him later), bad jails, bad health care and bad cops.

Chapter 13

Unforgettable Swift Change

In the light of that August 2006 election upset, democratic rule simply delivered appropriate swift change. Relying on a whole lot of sense and just enough action, Roane Citizens saved the day. They asked for strong government and a commanding sheriff.

As Roane toppled county government on the heels of the Houstons' crime, the press forwarded the response across the state. When law officers are gunned down in two separate incidents just months apart, with the first taking place in a public parking lot at the foot of the courthouse steps, people everywhere want to know what went wrong. They also seek solutions to outlawed behavior before it becomes rife where they live.

Now, those winning officials knew they had a lot to accomplish. Replacing their disgraced predecessors propelled them to local prominence. Outwardly, the victorious district attorney general and new sheriff might have looked pleased. Nevertheless, expectations for them were high. Privately, they knew they must prosecute each case with gusto. It also fell on their shoulders to turn around numbers of staunch unruly attitudes. No county can survive when heckling malcontents lead the posse.

Past history caused those old timers to predict that "this will last for years." The newly elected needed to get beyond any expected long term aftermath. Such insane possibilities would stymie local government and discourage progressive public agendas. But the feuding continued with pickups and family sedans posting bumper stickers that unabashedly broadcast "We

Support the Houstons" and "Remember Bill Jones." The divided camp's foot stomping anger sustained itself. Some could only see Rocky and Leon as conquering heroes, and others remembered the men they had killed.

Of course their prolonged pre-trial motion hearings gave the Houstons plenty of face time in their continual trips to the Roane County Court House. The essential requirement of providing the criminals with a fair trial was adroitly handled by retired Anderson County Judge James "Buddy" Scott who was steeled with strength. Sternly and patiently abiding their loud and loutish remarks had to play hard on him as he retained a courtly composure. One didn't have to look at the safety restraints the admitted killers wore to court to get the serious picture. Their faces accomplished that. Unrestricted looks at them divulged their temperaments. Scott's own face weathered a bit over time. He remained their concrete pin cushion and courtroom purist as they attempted to disobey and take charge of him and his courtroom.

Leon's face kept its stoic, craggy look. He seemed to look inward instead of outward. He froze out strangers. That head to shoulders was as stone cold as a plaster bust. No suit and tie or good lawyering would work to change his bad man portrait.

On the other hand, if brother Rocky honestly looked himself square in the face, he should have been frightened. Cornered and captured, he was a nightmare of a man. It would be easy to look away. Some felt his wife Nancy, stayed with him out of pity; others felt differently. His looks alone were controlling, the kind of looks that demanded submission.

Both men's visages grew larger as the pre-trial appointments added up to years. Leon, the physically larger of the two, sweated danger. The never-settled Rocky could not have survived without the intimidation of his large, very large weapons. He proved to be a little man with a big mouth. Those two pieces of the family puzzle, even when surrounded by SWAT team members, provoked fear. The combination did not speak well for humanity. Still those long sculpted terrifying expressions required at least a second look, even a stare. That is as long as the scary men were shackled. Normal people needed to know what grew such wicked countenances.

Oh my. Requesting new bonds, they told the judge they wanted to go back to normal lives. Normal to them would not have been normal to many. Normal was not going to happen in their lifetimes. Did they have any idea of what they were saying? Their nine hundred thousand dollar bonds per man held firm.

If a push came to a shove, some of those who knew possibilities felt that they should have been secured away from others in the courtroom. Kept in an adjacent room to attend their hearing via a television hook up, the raucous circus would have been cut to the chase for formal courtroom business only.

The public scrapbook that followed the required procedures showed them led and watched by weapon laden guards in formidable bullet proof attire. Canines with handlers stood close. They were now cuffed, instead of carrying cuffs whose prior use even had been to threaten a sitting judge. Back "when" they were the ones wearing body armor. They liked the look. Being on the other side of this show of force must have been hard for them to swallow.

Rocky, with or without a lawyer, took the lead. During such continued court inquiries, he beamed, became hot headed, and shouted out charges. He tried his recusal trick unsuccessfully on Judge Scott and acted like a perturbed windup toy. Coming and going from the courthouse, he always turned to get the last word for the cameras. Most often he shouted out a backlash of his worn conspiracy theory repertoire. In the end there were benefits to recognizing what the Houstons' victims had to tolerate for years. For the time being, those who had been outside of Rocky's world were invited in.

The boys' earliest request following their charges of felony murders was to remove the Roane's district attorney general. Nonsense again. The countywide election had already done that. But, without hesitation, these far-reaching complainers fell back upon their laddered and repeated lawsuits. Other local, state, and United States government officials needed to be removed. Same ol' same ol': Their enemies had participated in fraud and conspiracy against them. Indeed they knew how to turn an accusation inside out to portray themselves differently. Again and again, they had to have believed their own paper harassment against the courts would be a red badge of courage. Such success attributed to others should eventually come to them.

Digging out of this mess was not easy. And it had taken a caucus to bring in retired Judge Scott and Robert "Gus" Radford, esteemed Tennessee District Attorney General and lecturer (also retired), to prosecute the Roane County extremists. Having waited so long to take on the Houston nightmare, the decision was smart. Roane knew it needed outside legal minds with broad shoulders to accept the daunting task. The local list had been exhausted. Over the years, the brothers Houston had reportedly sued every lawyer in Roane County, making them unacceptable in capacity or "fairness." Needless to conclude perhaps would be that the brothers never would consider they had been treated fairly. They had no idea of fair play.

These smart choices went with the changes in Roane County government. Here were jurists with sterling reputations who would not be recused. For years the Houstons demanded that lawyers and judges recuse themselves. They smilingly messed up their court appearances and the court dockets. No brilliance here, just rote behavior. And nothing new to any of those multiple other separatists groups out there who had led the way. The Houston two enjoyed a way of life that they had bootlegged from others.

It worked. The ploy became a habit: They continued their paper havoc; eliminated authority; and continued their criminal tomfoolery. Anti-government comrades in arms, according to The Southern Poverty Law Center, had successfully worked the larger system across the country.

As time for the planned July 14, 2008 trial moved closer, the legal cadre worked hard to sterilize trial procedure. Getting it right for a successful outcome meant everything. The reality of bogus or real complaints had to be considered.

And so, the course of action continued for the upcoming trial of the two charged with first degree/felony murders. The new Roane District Attorney General Russell Johnson went way west and north to Paris, Tennessee—just below the Kentucky border——to find a "Gus" Radford, the retired prosecutor with the sterling reputation, to work the case. Even pretrial hearings proceeded under the auspices of outside judges. Preparation was precise. The two brothers had fooled around with the justice system much too long. The state prepared to flex its muscle. The gold standard for them would be a prosecutorial conviction within an unencumbered trial.

By the time a grand jury had indicted the alleged killers, circumstances had ricocheted back to the duo. Poetic justice had Rocky and Leon, not their victims, "behind the gun." They got a long look at what might be now lying in wait for them.

Even within the community, which had rallied behind new government, it was doubtful any had an idea of how new that would be—at least as applied to the strategy taken to assure the Houstons of a fair trial. For certain, the public definitely had a time recognizing the legal eagles: new men in black robes and a new stateside prosecutor. They convened to get things pin perfect.

Ironically, the Houstons got their dream team—even as it pointed to the gathered judges and the prosecution: Not one of those selected had ever had direct dealings with the accused. Of course Rocky never liked lawyers. Never wanted one. He still didn't.

The youngest Mr. Houston believed he was as good as any lawyer and better than most. Goodness, just how far could narcissism mislead a man? Still, either his vanity or mental liabilities drove him onward. His reputation went on as he raged against and fired lawyers. He wanted to be his own lawyer. He wanted to talk out directly to the judge at his pleasure. He wanted to be "the man."

Randy Rogers from the small town of Athens, Tennessee came forward initially as Rocky's attorney. The cycle of hiring and firing may have been a ploy to keep the Houstons out of the hot seat. It definitely looked that way.

And of course Rocky didn't get the $7 million he sued Rogers for. Hired, fired, and hired again. Is this how bullies act when they get caught?

Pro se, no say, Rocky strutted his stuff. Legal texts might even recognize him one day. He could teach yet unconvinced law students of what they could be up against.

Actually, according to those who should know, the Houstons kept pushing merit-less paper onto the U.S. Court's Eastern District for the entire two years. Then publicly, the Court said enough is enough and refused to accept more from them. Looking into the faces of superior knowledge at the high court level never seemed to dissuade the two militants from believing they were neck and neck in winning an argument with the law of the land.

Incarcerated Rocky continued to file his complaints in his combative style until he was stopped. Regardless of his fixed position behind bars, he settled well into that lawsuit routine, believing he had a hand on the law forever. Time will tell if that is true. Given a trial outcome, light source, and writing instrument, there is probably nothing that will stop Rocky Houston's creative but hollow written arguments. Maybe this self-taught trade will keep him occupied the rest of his life.

Chapter 14

The Law Soldiers On

Even if given the right opportunity and circumstances, it would have taken miracles to have stopped entirely the Houston momentum prior to the double homicides. And a glimpse back focused on the need for local law enforcement to see it through. But the word of law usually holds to a virtuous card hand. It did here when up against the co-dependent Houston men. Here cool heads and lawyer combatants quietly and fearlessly continued. They did what they were justified to do: go after the bad guys. That works in the long run because most often villains get their final justice. The legal establishment and the arm of the law did their best to untangle the mounting nightmare lying in wait. It escalated anyway.

Taking on the job as the law's messengers (to include cops, deputies, attorneys or judges) can be a dangerous and often grim business, even for a nation built on the rule of law. Citizens depend on such people. They do get killed. During 2006, the year-of-the Houstons, 151 officers were killed while on duty. Attorneys and judges face much the same.

Apparently, the men the Houstons killed were seen as couriers as they rode into "Houston territory." Their routine job defended their trip there. But riding in a car marked Roane County Sheriff's patrol ended it for them. The job and the car added up to a paradigm of all the Houstons hated. The roving mostly unemployed brothers' lawsuits named better known, even nationally known, enemies. But not one of those big names was slumped dead in the car adjacent to the Houston homestead.

Violent criminals, according to social psychologist Richard Rhodes, "decide to act violently based on their interpretation of the situation." Kingston folks, like most, needed little professional help to secure that part of the Rhodes' conclusion. Yet, during the years and years of Houston lawsuits and conspiracy theories, some of the public were unaware of their inherent violence. Those who most often had to deal with them knew the full conclusion could include murder and mayhem. Community nightmares can be kept lying in wait for years. Confronting such recognized nightmares takes more than cops.

So, the biting question in this piece of skullduggery did not conclude with a "whodunit?" Maybe not even a "why?" The question left dangling was who might have atrophied the Houston behavior? As of now, a look around might help.

Commonly it is community which eliminates early years of misdemeanors, petty assaults, and miles of crime. Surprisingly it seemed to work differently with Rocky and Leon who lived closely to a large extended family, neighborhood schools, and church upbringing.

Each institution can nip bad behavior in the bud. They can be the solution. And that old fashioned thinking doesn't and shouldn't be cruel or violent—just evenhanded versus backhanded. Actually, all three groups can combine to bring about good childhood and adolescent development. At least they can try. Without a vaccine to wither spiraling bad behavior, these groups stand tall.

The first government that children recognize is at home. Eventually that spreads to schools and churches. But big doses of justice are hard to hand out by those who occasionally stand against those they love. After all, humans perceive a bit of their own immortality in their offspring. They generally want them to turn out well.

At home, parents are known to tell kids that the punishment hurts the parents more than it does the children. And they aren't speaking of beatings. Often it means taking away privileges that cause the entire family to miss an event in order to stay at home to supervise the punishment. What parent can impose restrictions when he or she isn't there to see that those terms and conditions are enforced?

An educator's classroom management instruction can serve as another noteworthy possibility. Teachers know the prosecution of gum chewing (or that of any minor rule) does a lot to resolve later disciplinary necessities. If the teacher says "no" immediately to small offences, students learn misconduct's limits. Quick to enforce an even minor infraction, a teacher can take control of the unruly for the rest of the year. The simplest strategies at home and at school prove to make a difference. But even the best parents can fall into believing their children have been harassed. Sometimes they are right. It can be true. Most often it isn't true; and, those parents pay the ultimate price with future tears and broken dreams.

Churches can put forth a lexicon of spiritual and literal knowledge that can never be and shouldn't be digested in one setting. It can begin with sweet music, comforting prayers and angels' wings. The association with the goodness and hope of religious thinking can stand as a help mate for eternity.

Now totalitarian, cruel, and violent measures in any of the above have proven defeating and often illegal in their own right. But straightforward rule enforcement holds as a governing duty. That government begins at home, moves to schools and churches, and ends up with the law. By the time the law steps in it will take some harsh measures to turn that bad behavior around.

Keeping ahead of crime is essential in order to prevent civilized freedom erupting into chaos. Recent FBI crime statistics published by the New York Times show that the biggest cities seem to be the ones successfully fighting crime. The reason behind the study equates to what The Times' Bob Herbert calls "enlightened policing," where cops share their information and just get smarter because of it. Of course, Roane County's new guys on the block had known about information sharing. The local police chiefs in Kingston, Rockwood, Harriman, Oak Ridge, and Oliver Springs were well connected to that professional "enlightenment." They were ready for change, and didn't take their responsibility loosely.

People hung their hopes on one man's promises when they elected Jack Stockton sheriff August 3rd, 2006. A gathering for "Jackie," the earlier Harriman chief, took place election eve at Kingston's First Baptist Church. Victory smiles and handshakes brought together burdensome memories.

Some in the crowd cited ex-sheriff Haggard's lack of enthusiasm for the work ethic. As one woman reported, several in Sheriff Haggard's office claimed "the guy had shown up to work late and left early." And then comments weighed in again on that other deadly crime scene that didn't have to occur in March of 2006 outside the courthouse.

In this case, Wayne "Cotton" Morgan, a popular guard at Tennessee's Brushy Mountain State Prison was gunned down as he prepared to take a prisoner into the county building for a court hearing. He died in the parking lot. The inmate and his wife Jennifer Hyatte took off. Fortuitously, the homicide and escape occurred just months before the deaths of Jones and Brown. Rumors abounded then that, fairly or unfairly, the Sheriff at the time of the deadly courthouse escape couldn't be found anywhere—that is until hundreds of news media rolled into Roane. His accusers say they saw it that way then and now.

That hard to forget criminal flight to escape, with plenty of spectators dangerously close to the action, begged questions of proper precautions. The Sheriff's office stood adjacent to the same parking lot. Somehow updated precautions had never been taken. Unloading convicts in such a public location, with or without proper backup, truly was unimaginable. That naivety needed to be buried and changed. But it appears that this Sheriff's naiveté also pointed back to his management of the Houstons.

The prisoner and his compatriot wife, like Bonnie and Clyde, ran fast and far. As the story swept the national news, the Sheriff himself took some hits. No doubt, a lack of proficient planning had contributed to the break. They were eventually cornered in Ohio and sentenced to prison terms. Mrs. Hyatt will be in prison for life without parole.

Not surprisingly, persistent questions accumulated when law enforcement gathered to hunt down the Houstons. They too fled from the homicide scene they were accused of bringing about. It seemed fair to question how much the Sheriff's long term lagging cooperation had contributed to Rocky's and Leon's brazen deadly behavior. Indeed, the resolve to stand behind his oath to serve and protect Roane's citizens seemed to have weakened. The prisoner George Hyatte's escape along with the help of his wife, followed by the deaths of a Roane deputy and his ride-along, took down several top officials when the people spoke in the 2006 election. The citizens stood strong for change.

Weeks prior to the election, the widely read local news columnist Gerald Largen effectively pared down the problems of county government. Largen, a well-recognized attorney, designated the then District Attorney General Scott McCluen a cameo role, if not a humorous role, in his published critiques. Although a favorite critic, Largen was not alone. Chis Cawood, also lawyer and author, spewed his own dramatic vitriol at Roane's McCluen. Friends of McCluen apparently stayed on the sidelines.

While the topic of bad government had won the day, the new government had taken on its own burdens: The Houston storm clouds and other lawless attitudes waited. It would take a lot of rain to extinguish clashing old school and new school law enforcement methodologies.

To many, evidence was rife: professional police training required additional revenue; methamphetamine labs grew; and rural hamlets could not be islands unto themselves.

South of Kingston the old culture was awash in "immigrants": New comers and part-time residents from "off" kept buying the lush landscape along and above the Tennessee River. And while they built their mini mansions, they also replaced old names attached to once forceful power structures. The local pleasure of taking the law into your own hands also would have to go.

Book Two:

When They Became the Houstons

Chapter 15

A Far Cry from Old Ed Houston

Living memories of "old Ed," grandfather to the infamous brothers Houston, provide happy references to their kin: Ed, a man of stature, was a highly praised and admired patriarch. Aging men and women recall Ed and his wife sitting on the front porch in picture perfect terms. The two nodded friendly greetings from a home that was somewhat solitary. As the family grew and stayed, the landscape took on a nest of Houston family homes. Today that same house where Leon had recently lived has a defining number: 412 Barnard Narrows. Today the Houston landmark is more conspicuously ear marked as a recent crime scene. Picturesque no longer tells its story.

Grandfather Ed was a genial man. According to verbal histories, men would gather to talk on Ed's wrap-around porch about politics or evolving community issues. On other occasions it was a place of tranquility for fellow gentleman farmers. He didn't have to go far with this leadership status; people came to him.

Clyde followed his father Ed to some extent, but in a more public light. Ed's son seemed to walk in his father's amiable footsteps. He formalized that path when he was elected for one term as county commissioner to represent his South of the River district. Clyde, as was true of his dad, had good standing at home and a good name across the county.

Now, nostalgic flashbacks might forfeit part of such a historic pedigree. In recent years Mr. Rocky Houston's and Mr. Leon Houston's bad names have put a different face on the legacy. Their recent alleged double felony murders attached to their attacks on multi-levels of government spewed disrepute all over the bloodline.

Going back to courthouse records, the earliest Roane County Houstons come to life. According to Roane County records, they resettled there in 1934. Those family members traveled a bit south when eminent domain forced them from their Union County land in preparation for the Tennessee Valley Authority's Norris Dam and Norris Lake. Conceptualized in 1929, TVA embarked on projects that provided electric power across the southern United States ultimately spurring progress. This meant industrial development, jobs, and even the eventually attached harbinger of change: air-conditioning! Monumentally it made the South's hot summers hospitable. Libraries and librarians were an ancillary outcome like never before: electricity in no small way delivered light for reading.

The earliest Roane Houstons were W.M. and John F., along with their wives Alice and Sarah, stately names, evident of the times and traditional mores. Ambitious as well: They bought, farmed, and successfully held onto large land parcels, which ultimately would pass to their kin.

Clearly, the TVA initiated a certain semblance of hope to those states defeated and languishing for years following what some in the South called the "War of Northern Aggression." Although the war itself ended in 1865— it was sixty-four years before such progress beneath the Mason-Dixon Line began.

Tennesseans, disruptively divided turning America's Civil War, held a long term memory of their losses. After all, Tennessee inadvertently had provided the great battleground between North and South. Roane County's memory, like most counties of East Tennessee, held fast to the corruptive loss that permanently had split neighbors and brothers, and also launched years of economic retribution. So, when the United States Government initiated the TVA, the plan was generally welcome by most. Its entrance into the region turned heads away from the division of the past toward the promises of the future.

With federally sponsored progress, Norris Dam became Tennessee's first hydro-electric dam and power plant. So it was that the early Houstons' historic background put a stamp on Rocky and Leon Houston's lives:

As the homes of W. M. and Alice and John F. and Sarah fell beneath the flooding waters of the dam, they built others in the area now known by the United States' Post Office as Ten Mile, Tennessee, and more widely known as part of the sturdy community designated colloquially as "South of the River." The Houston family tree cultivated the land and gained salvation while following the Biblical instruction to work "by the sweat of your brow." As suggested by the good Christian theology of early Americans, work within itself was rewarding. And the family must have worked hard and often to clear the land and make the acreage productive.

At first sight, protected and geographically fenced somewhat by towering "Bacon Ridge," this farmland and these homes provide a picture book commune similar to Iowa's once widely recognized Amana communities of the 1920's and 30's. Here and then, their ambitious nature and hard-work joined to present today's lingering appearance of homespun interdependence and industry. Ruggedly the Houston clan's family lifestyle captures the visitor's imagination. Minds yearning for scenic roads and sacred values would surely be fulfilled with a Sunday afternoon drive there. But from 2006 on, almost anyone in law enforcement would have discouraged that particular sentimental journey. There were definitely warning shots back in those mountains that discouraged interest in the Houstons or the Houston property.

One thing is certain: Whether they liked it or not, the Houston family's 1930's move had not eliminated their distance from the federal government's reach. And, by the 1990's the infamous brothers Houston's hostility to government had not gone cloaked or hidden.

Their anger against the government described in their pro-se lawsuits added nothing to their personal lives but instead seems to have taken life away from them. This self approached legal channel must also have bled the emotions of local, state, and federal courts on a frequently occurring basis.

The pro-se lawsuits written and presented by the Houstons took hold of their lives and the federal and local courts' routines. The complainants' monotonous recurring themes contained a rash of personal anti-government attacks. Most often without a lawyer's help, their tracts went ahead with both written and oral missteps.

It was not without cost. Most people would see the continuous need to file lawsuits (whether in local or federal courts) as an expensive habit: Specific fees must be paid to the clerk for filing; there is the expense of serving subpoenas; the petitioner is charged for the summons or notice to defendants; court transcripts must be paid for; and there is a price for copying papers or exhibits. All of this quickly can mount to hundreds, even thousands of dollars.

Eventually, two under-employed men paid for their paper blitz. The justice system also paid a price. There, tax payers paid employees to sort through the rugged twosomes' work products.

The two men built a lengthy repertoire of these preposterous personal and paper appearances in Knoxville's Federal Courthouse. The Ten Mile two's contributions stalled government and wrinkled brows. Ironically so, their failed messages gave them purpose; in that way they proved successful.

The two government opponents continued openly to condemn the system. Still few people outside of the court system had ever read even one page of their paper pushing enterprise. If they had, they might have seen an ulterior motive behind what appeared to be ridiculous lawsuits. They might have recognized that they could not apply their past Houston memories to the brothers. The past was the past.

Chapter 16

Homebound Boys to Men

At home, law enforcement had a reason to know the Houston two up close and personal for years. They stood guard for good reason. At home the two vocalized their opinions and antagonized the police. An example of this was when Jack Stockton, then a young Harriman officer, disarmed Rocky at Food City in Harriman. Stockton was shopping there with his wife. He glimpsed Rocky carrying an unconcealed gun on his hip as he loitered about in the store's aisles. Stockton told his wife to go to the back of the store so that she would be safe when he approached the man. He didn't know him. But he thought someone was up to no good; and, at that time he did not know how well he would get to know him. Then and there he disarmed him. The outcome of this action brought an immediate surprise or two with it.

After taking Rocky outside of the store, he verified through the sheriff's office that the Ten Mile resident had a gun carry (concealed weapon) permit—somewhat new at the time. Stockton acknowledged the fact and gave him back his gun. Rocky then laughingly told him that he had another gun on him anyway. He immediately revealed the one in an ankle holster. This is the mindset that eventually led to openly wearing body armor.

How could anyone miss that the Houstons liked playing with the law? Certainly a few thought that the Houston brothers' overreaching court ambitions might one day tender violence. Beneath the surface the psychology of Rocky's and Leon's gamesmanship sent out a message or two. Overheated personalities that aggressively challenge the rules quite often destroy themselves or others.

Even facts not associated with the Houstons' behavior shed light on their circumstances. According to Dr. Randy Dupont, psychologist at the University of Memphis, textbook theory addresses behavior resulting from either depression or anger: "Depression can, at times, be displaced by anger." The idea goes forward to explain that depression can hold a person in place, while anger can push him to act. Both possibilities are better off dealt with on the spot. Instead, all possibilities here lay in wait.

Since mental health professions were not injected early into the mix, little exists that can support the thinking. And the Houston defense never went that direction. Judge James "Buddy" Scott who listened closely to their courtroom uproar wanted to know. Both, on Scott's orders, were tested more than once and were found competent to stand trial. And previous psychological profiles done by mental health professionals had never pointed to depression or anger. Relying on such information, it looks as if they, at anytime, could have made an abrupt turn away from their risky behavior.

On the other hand no one looked beyond the obvious. No one connected their behavior with similar anti-government participants. There were and are an acknowledged myriad of cult movements in America. Such anti-government groups help others establish their positions, conspiracies, and courtroom tricks. Most of it is done underground.

Without money and prolonged undercover investigations these small groups thrive. Now and then just enough inspiration can spring from reading and upholding "common law court" diatribe. The ideas are available on the internet, but were more popular fifteen years ago than they are now. After 9/11, domestic terrorism took a back seat, even though recorded information from the investigation of the Oklahoma Bombing took some of that thinking outside of the United States.

So it goes that the "common law court" advocates believe that if you can't have your way with the sheriff, you should kill him. In this anarchist theory, the only government to which one should give allegiance is county government. That isn't just any county government, but a county government of which such movements hope to take control. Separatist groups waver a bit between tenets of belief systems. They do not waver on their overall anti-government beefs. What a fraternity!

One thing for sure is that the Houstons used the Internet—citing, in fact, a legal help web cite in at least one law suit. Acquaintances also stand behind the fact that Rocky had enthusiasm for the internet; they confirm his pointed interest in establishing his own web cite.

According to criminal justice guidelines there was little the law could do to stop the Houstons. Of course their inclination to "flee" from outstanding warrants against them handed the police the opportunity to curb their unruly nature. Sadly, many onlookers saw even the simplest procedures to rein them in as police harassment.

Subversive by choice, the brothers were not to be managed. They seem to have held close the obstinacy of their adolescence. They countered fact with opinion even in school. Teachers know that someone who already "knows" can seldom learn.

Begging not to be quoted, some of the Houston family themselves said that Clyde Houston's sons for years had acted "stark crazy." Family was family, and these same people silently suffered the boys' nutty bullying tactics. In Ten Mile, Rocky's and Leon's law had weight.

Then on May 11th all of that "government" for the Houstons and by the Houstons jelled in blood. And if anyone believed these horrific deaths had finalized the sporting game of legal maneuvers, grandstanding and conspiracy theories, they were just as deadly wrong.

But before the brothers would be judged by a jury of their peers for first degree felony murders, Rocky and Leon would get a lot more face time during courtroom motion hearings and news coverage. If earlier they had acquired a faux celebrity, it quickly turned to martyrdom. A growing number of clueless followers bought into the myth, giving them their continuing wish to be recognized.

From boys to men, they floundered between destinations. Leon in 1975 and then Rocky in 1976 entered high school, graduating in 1978 and 1979. They were different to a degree, as to how they kept their skewed attitudes public. They were rough and often negative; threatening but not criminally so. Differently, most of their male Midway High associates were country boys, proud to serve right over might. Those kids took straight paths to become upstanding people. The twosome chose a different course—together.

Although their fellow students all lived a distance from town, few of them missed recognizing their generation's coming of age: fast cars, leisure suits and disco. Whether young people grew up in New York or South of the River, the popular film *Saturday Night Fever*, 1977, portrayed their interests and age group. Probably known to them was the music of *Lynyard Skynryd*, *Aerosmith*, and *Earth, Wind and Fire*; contemporaries in Kingston report that they did. And if they were not the youths cavorting in flares and bell bottoms, they knew many others who took up the style. Much of America worked to look away from the nation's painful losses at the Vietnam War's end. Television helped sustain that need with popular programs like *The Brady Bunch and The Partridge Family*.

Yet beneath it all, Roane County had inherited a sweeping culture of its own. While Midway High's 1979 yearbook listed the Houstons' cousin Starlin Yates by his nickname "moonshiner," Rocky faired only somewhat better with his nickname "dirt." Definitely both had labels to forget. And with the intervention of time, most bygone friends forgot both names and boys.

A few football teammates do recall Rocky's moniker "dirt." Football was his only high school sport, and the expression "dig it" must have applied to his enthusiasm for the game. Although reminiscences about that name were vague, a few portrayed him spending a lot of athletic time on the ground. Who really knows? Many old acquaintances wanted to forget they ever knew Rocky—even before the double homicides.

Almost everyone remembered him as somewhat of a bully, and a guy who back then had a hair trigger attitude. Even early, they knew both brothers were different from their small community of young people.

Time and time again, those who responded agreed that Rocky's steady complaint about others "out to get his family" seemed peculiar. Now it would be questioned. Today people would ask if it could have been a developing paranoia. The term then was not yet part of the public's lexicon.

Today the psychological term is loosely used to describe a fearfully harvested mistrust of others' behavior. But whatever the trait, the peculiarity eventually particular to both brothers never changed during the next 27 years. Of course, if these accounts are valid, such mental health signals beg the question: Did any professional think the combination of mistrust and bad temper were worth looking into?

Much needed attention then and now is halted by student privacy issues. And still suggestions for mental health testing or acknowledgement of such problems still would have been vehemently deterred. In all fairness, a lot of staggering personalities begin at home and can end there. Faulty family dynamics are commonly corrected or overcome in the privacy of their own homes.

Not everything suggested a slippery slope ahead in those Midway yearbooks. Aside from a quarrelsome attitude, Rocky Houston was likely recognized in his seventeenth year as red-neck cute, looking a bit like the character "Bo" on the popular 70's TV program *The Dukes of Hazzard*. Rocky's blonde hair, parted in the middle, covered his ears with curls and sunshine scrubbed his broad, bright smile.

Along this memory lane, a yearbook photo proudly records him and football teammate Ronnie Hackworth escorting the 1979 Homecoming Queen. Both graduating seniors beamed as they looked out to the applauding crowd.

A closer look at Rocky's photographs and standing may reveal a small part of his aggressive persona, which in the end became his undoing: There is undeniably a glint of cocky in that picture. Since a few remaining faculty look back to remember his hot temper, it would be fair to identify a bit of that hostile nature attaching itself to the revealing self-important satisfaction of the photo. Fairly put, males tend to lose that aggressive nature with age. Neither Houston brother conformed to the statistical expectations.

Consensus has it that as Rocky aged he had difficulty handling his undeniable need to become irritated: In the end, it appears that his fury would get the best of him. But seldom does a community know how to handle such disturbing hostility set behind a Colgate smile. Customarily the law inherits the problem.

Older bubba Clifford Leon, known to every one as Leon and not Clifford, graduated from Midway High just one year ahead of Rocky. Then, and in their futures, they always were closer than close. Leon did not participate in sports, but spent two years with the Future Farmers of America. Across the country, males in farm families joined the FFA. Girls joined the Future Homemakers of America, or FHA. Both now are open to either gender.

Many of Leon's fellow 1978 classmates showed more interest in school clubs and activities than he did. He carried the nickname "Crash." And "Crash" grew to be known as an almost engaging man until he began to buttonhole individuals on his deeply felt but confusing religious invectives. More often he was labeled as a "doper," with at least one early Kingston drug arrest. His confrontational approach grew to make people nervous. He may have liked himself full of advice better than the less definable but shadowy "Crash" of his past. As life went on, people claim Leon took his uncomfortable image as a man into drugs and mayhem to the limit. Known around as "the biggest bad ass" in the valley, he may have enjoyed his reputation. Knowingly or unknowingly, he created this one without the help of Rocky Joe.

As he approached and passed forty, even the young people who encountered him thought him strange. After acting "loony," in confrontations with them, he would politely back off with a "God bless you." With older folks he displayed the same quirky aggressive behavior. In actuality, as reported, both men were picking up the pace of their outlandish clashes. And as the conduct isolated them more, they converted into a duality which alarmed people.

But when pushed to interpret the brother who provided the precarious momentum, the younger adults believed Leon was the one that authorities should have been watching—not Rocky. Differently, the older crowd saw Rocky as "half-baked." What a tag team they had become.

Leon's nature gained speed as he spewed venom against people in government to captive audiences. He assured them that both brothers were just trying to save the world; in fact he encouraged his audience the necessity of doing the same for their children. None of that sounded too original. Again, small-minded cult leaders had had such thinking out there and available for years. And it was during such encounters that the least verbal of the brothers assailed the wide-eyed with his opinions. Suddenly self-conscious or feeling rejected, Leon then would hastily back out of his own adrenalin spills, bestowing his repeated blessings from God on those he had cornered. Especially confusing was the religious oratory of his farewells. To his neighbors, his reputed drug worship was ungodly and had replaced no part of the Holy Trinity. Perhaps there was someone who recognized Rocky or Leon as their own victims calling out for help. On the other hand no male or female close enough to suggest such a perspective ever did so. They knew better than to voice such an idea. Lives were at stake.

If these well known facts were expected to go away they did not until they festered into murder. A semblance of peace came to those whose homes were across the river while the tireless two were locked up. But even behind bars, the community was lying in wait. Many voiced the fear that they would one day be set free.

More and more South of the River citizens admitted having known Leon for the heralded and "kooky" manner in which he approached them; both brothers were known for their meanness. And who could believe following the "killings" that men would congregate to discuss "taking up" money for Clyde? Of course they sympathized with the men's father—knowing the price of their criminal defense would fall back on the Houston patriarch.

After the fact, the brothers' most strident differences came forward: Leon was unmarried while Rocky was married with children. His children lived at home. Both of Rocky's children must have become victims as well.

Rocky's daughter will never forget her high school graduation planned for May 12th. Had Rocky and Leon forgot to mark the calendar? Due to her dad's and uncle's overt behavior, things changed quickly. Midway High's graduation was postponed: Her dad was in the hospital and, at that point, charged with murder. Her uncle was on the run. Her high school had become a law enforcement command post. It couldn't have been much worse. Not surprisingly, it was reported that Rocky's girl had to be urged to participate when the ceremony took place on the 13th.

The school previously filled with senior pride suddenly became lost to perimeter blue lights and those congregated to investigate the crime scene. The Houston's personal history couldn't be overlooked. This school was the same country school from which both men had graduated more than twenty-five years earlier. Other Houston family as well had sung the school's song and reached for their ribbon bound diplomas on graduation day. Rocky's younger son was to return there as a student in the fall. The kid was already brittle at best, missing many earlier days of the school year. One would be remiss to neglect the fact that Rocky's wife Nancy provided some stability for her children and stayed employed at a Kingston bank.

Leon lived alone. He operated as a loner in most ways, but was the one who had been bequeathed the homestead. His high school portrait in his 1970's bow tie projects discomfort. This man seems to be a guy who would depend on Rocky's more confident social skills. Leon never married, but had a recent relationship with a woman who believed in him and his more private behavior.

Perhaps, in the same sense, their agenda was not that different from the scripted plot of *"The Dukes of Hazzard."* In fictional Hazzard County, Georgia, Bo and his brother Luke held together an ongoing war with the sheriff. There the Duke boys ran moonshine in violation of the law, which did not go unnoticed. As the plot centered on their ability to laugh at "the law," the Houston brothers' comparable anti-government behavior inserts itself into the somewhat similar story: In both cases, "the boys" go after other government officials who they believe are participants in public corruption, or just plain "out to get them."

Strangely enough, *"The Dukes of Hazzard"* was considered a lifestyle comedy, born and bread at home in Tennessee's neighboring Georgia. If these homegrown Houston men were ever funny like the sitcom, they had lost their edge to tragic endings. Even worse, they ended the life stories of the men they killed. Harder to accept, the dead men's families saw the deceased names come to be buried beneath the hoop-la that gave the Houstons' story life. That story only served to give the remaining status to the alleged killers.

Chapter 17

Different Game Board

Of course while the police chiefs fought crime, Rocky and Leon were on the opposing side of that game board: They pushed crime. To some it seemed that way. To some it didn't. On the sidelines the Houston believers grew into what became an uninformed but supportive constituency, uninformed on the law but faithful to the agitator's explanations of it.

How strikingly unbelievable it was to watch as the community's turmoil lay in wait: over two years and two deaths later it remained unsettled. High bonds holding the terrible two in separate jails during two years of pre-trail work were not sufficient to rid the community of turmoil. The press could not manage to keep them out of sight or out of mind. Their own repugnant behavior could not be ignored. It definitely was unseemly.

The sum total of clearly defined rules would not hold the center against the disruptive Houston crowd. As poet William Butler Yeats explains: "When the centre cannot hold, things fall apart." The neighborhood that knew the rules for a civil community hung on silently—waiting behind as things did fall apart. The fury of the discontent continued and divided those who spoke out. The Judge himself started to look distraught as he tried to hold the center. The need for such a good man to stand up to the brothers Houstons 'gyrating forces seemed cruel and inhuman. On most hearing days the public tyrants looked like two men inflicted with the "screaming memes." In Rocky's case, he made a habit of inflicting an emotional debris field on the court.

The legion aligned with the Houstons had itself had for years held close to their own. One native says it doesn't even matter if someone marries into a family South of the River; that person who moves here is never really one of us. Among many, it is "my neighbors right or wrong." Change was the devil in disguise. With the global world changing faster than citizens anywhere seemed to accept, perhaps this was a small but an exact example about such pain. These people seemed to desperately believe they could hold onto the past. So, if it took the Houston's to fight their insecurities, why not let them do it?

So predictably, even the Houstons' prison stripes shouted like cheerleaders to many South of the River. Rocky's and Leon's reputation grew; and as it did, the alleged killers continued to undergo romantic face lifts— icons of sorts. Whether that was due to "outlaw cool" or sympathy related to their long perceived harassment claims, their public was there for them.

Prior to the murders there was more and more talk about how badly the Houstons had been treated. Sources knowledgeable said Rocky, the talker of the two, went from place to place with plenty of fodder to keep that flame burning. For certain, he cunningly sought the public's desire to romanticize him as a martyr.

Local funeral home owner Gail Brown said when the men's mother died, they had to skip the Kingston visitation: "They knew the sheriff would harass or hassle them if they went into town." The Houston politics was rampant.

Knowledgeable others, thinking differently, ridiculed the men's popularized diatribe. They recognized the neighborhood group's underdeveloped critical thinking. Even college students home visiting commented that a lot of those people are "outright loopy." For those who left home, they had never been asked to access their own "born and reared with" thinking. For a few, the counterculture waited for the evolving culture when they crossed the Tennessee River on the Highway 58 bridge.

Stuck with their copycat common law thinking against the sheriff, they overlooked the patience of both the old and the new sheriff who understood them better than they did themselves. Instead they became locked in to their thorny government prejudice.

While committed to looking at the "forest," the Ten Mile two never assessed the contributions of individual "trees," as in Shakespeare's *Macbeth*. Sheriff Haggard, it was often reported, inadvertently had been a tall timber in the Houston corner. Because of that omission they overlooked the surrounding huddle of area police chiefs who carefully monitored the "Ten Mile two come to town" behavior. Those worried law men who independently caucused recognized the team Houston couldn't be given much slack. But knowing didn't stop the pair from killing the men in the marked county cruiser.

Sorrowfully the friends regretted what could have been. They joined to look back at what they saw as the impetus that stood in the way: Emblematically, Rocky and Leon had too much time to plan their battle. The Sheriff's distance from the others thinking seemed to have sealed the bad boys' opportunity to build the excitement that never cooled down.

Soon after the dead men's funerals, the grape vine professed the same errors. There people said "it wasn't Sheriff Haggard that caused them trouble; it was Jackie Stockton." And now he was the new sheriff in town. Many citizens breathed a sigh of relief.

Perhaps other troublesome folks needed to go looking for another place to call home.

Chapter 18

Matched Against the Feds

The Houstons took their sport to the United States Federal Court for more than a decade, before few knew of their high jinks. Only a handful would really know. People just do not sit at home and read court documents. Much of what went on operated under this radar screen of untold unread material. Whether or not the brothers' need to be noticed brought them gratification will have to be left to criminal psychiatrists. Records show that their behavior definitely accelerated with time. Repeatedly taking their loutish license to the imposing high court eventually did work against them: It disclosed their arrogant identity. Overall they had trapped themselves in an inflated self importance. Mistakenly, they looked to a superior opponent.

Faithfully and boldly they harassed the Court. Shamelessly they dispatched weightless accusations. Naturally they "paid no mind" to procedural rules. While earning a repeated reputation in the justice system, their work-a-day persecution of the government went unnoticed by most citizens. The brothers Houston surreptitiously wreaked their harassing havoc.

Although they claimed to be victims of harassment, the brothers Houston and those at the top knew better. Their scheme was transparent. But the justice system was backed into a corner. Judges, along with their support staff, seemed honor bound for years to read the indiscernible accusations at taxpayers' expense. Those being sued had to hire lawyers to answer the Houston charges.

Rocky and Leon must have been gleeful as they posted their prattle to the Fed's mail room. Their years of Complaints, upon arrival at the federal building in Knoxville, had to have sent waves of mental anguish across the beleaguered recipients. It would be easy to speculate that headache remedies there were kept just an arm's length away.

Even after becoming known as the "anti-government brothers," they were seldom cited for the content of their malicious treatises. Just the idea that they continued to fling failed paper at the court should have pointed the blame back at them. Indeed, explanations were always sent to their Barnard Narrows homes in reply to their complaints in the form of legal Answers. Those impressive clear clarifications returned to them by the court system would have stopped, perhaps embarrassed, less quarrelsome minds.

But the Ten Mile two had learned the lingo of harassment. They had become adept at unleashing the bandwagon effect on their loyal, but unthinking followers. And they became even better at propagandizing their carefully cloaked motivation of self-aggrandizement:

In any case, they were not great minds, nor original. The cultish Houstons copied behavior that had brought attention to other separatists. Evidently they found a "calling" and liked themselves. Not alone, anarchists and fanatics have sprouted across the globe. The Houstons might have known how such uncompromising movements thrive and grow. The publicity was there to teach them. They had devious methods and plans.

Even in their isolated circumstances, just plain ol' Rocky and Leon gained a perimeter of power over people South of the River. They also intimidated quite a few city folks here and there in East Tennessee with their loud rough style and absurd remarks. Not often do business owners beg not to be identified. People did because of their fear of Houston retaliation. Such behavior commonly prevailed in East Tennessee research—especially where ever the Houstons had ever paid a visit.

In the end the men jumped ahead to federal court while still in criminal court; believed they could make their own rules; and verbally dismissed authority. Imagine the two scalawags' laughter as they plotted hidden away down that country road in the hinterland. Comfy, cozy for them.

That tempestuous trip can be best explained in the details of isolated lawsuits to the United States District Court, Eastern District of Tennessee in Knoxville. From June 17, 2002 to August 18, 2006, plaintiffs Rocky and Leon Houston sent twelve pleadings to Knoxville. Their documents consistently list people they believe have participated in their fore drawn conclusions to conspiracy against them. Selectively, these twelve Houston lawsuits have been chosen in order to reveal the truth. They should give the details of the documents overwhelming effects.

An earnest reader will recognize what no one else will ever get close to learning. Perhaps this alone is why such material went unnoticed: Again who would choose to "keep book" on the Houston malcontents prior to the homicides? Whether or not the Houstons' lawsuits are the product of paranoia or busywork, one cannot clarify. Factually, there is no substance: each lawsuit reveals mere accumulated litter.

When crimes are questioned, motives are sought. But typically, a normal person can not attach reason to any crime. Confusing as the Houston brothers behavior becomes, their need for attention and their desire to succeed pushes the need to identify motives. In some circumstances, the brothers Houston seem to go looking for dollars. After years of putting themselves out on a limb, positive relief from their financial damages might have both rewarded and stopped them. And while they went about their tomfoolery, why not demand millions of dollars? But, nowhere could they dig up a path of evidence which would reap top dollar financial gains for them. There was just no coupon in the justice system to redeem for their bad behavior.

Then again, they surely did intend to tie up the law. Suing every lawyer and judge they wanted to eliminate from their path worked fairly well. According to lessons from somewhere, they sought to recuse each named lawyer's or judge's courtroom appearance.

So it goes: The Houston brothers busily worked to devastate the system with their bloated personalities and bloated demands. In person, not understanding the negative effects of their loud-mouthed confrontations, they exited their in-your-face assaults with a "yes, sir," "yes ma'am," or "God bless you." Cartoonish in manner, they believed they could exit these circumstances with a bit of Southern homespun hospitality. Their rustic efforts were the ill-thought solutions to their problem solving. Most likely, they were unaware that they had acted like rubes.

Dropping that first written legal pleading into the mail must have been accompanied by pride. No one could have ever missed Rocky's high energy levels. Left alone he might have self-destructed; but Leon seemed always there to help him. In a sense, Leon truly appears to have been his brother's keeper: Quiet most of the time, big brother "propped up" Rocky when ever he could. Between them, team Houston gathered enough speed to take on a life of its own. If they believed in little else, they believed in each other: Rocky, at times, looked like a cute energizer bunny, while Leon stood stationary as his bodyguard. And Leon held out a look that kills.

Now filing lawsuits seems fair and square. Asking the justice system to hear legal Complaints is what Americans do every day. But, getting as involved as the brothers did carries uncharacteristic meaning. Seldom lucid, the combined lawsuits lead to the dead men on Barnard Narrows. The

Houstons longed to be believable. And they believed they could win in some manner or other.

Folks loyal to these men still subscribe to the Houston claim that they were victims of a harassing, scheming government. Yet none of these accusatory points connect to bring value to Mr. and Mr. Houston's conspiracy theories. Reasonable people find them odd, and dismiss the anti-government uproar. It wasn't as if East Tennessee didn't have their number. The rumor mill recognized them and chuckled. Of course through the rumor mill, they did become victims of developing chuckles. They were strange. Working their lawsuits must have become addictive. Somehow the brothers seem to have settled on a life in a pro se law practice of Houston and Houston. People with similar life long ambitions could only be found behind concertina wire. If they knew where this would take them, then they got what they wanted.

Their cloistered habitat helped. Believing what they believed would take isolation. When they weren't in their pick-up truck mailing subpoenas, or on the steps of the Federal Courthouse, they ran home to face-off with the law. The citizens group which believed the law had been soft on them blamed the system for creating two developing monsters. Conversely, their associates kept up with almost anything that made the bad boys appear as victims. The talking point of whether or not Rocky's and Leon's habitual behavior grew to their advantage would never be settled. It definitely supplied them with a fighting stance. They thrived on the underdog propaganda.

In court, they were legally and intellectually in far over their heads. Most of the time they continued to go forth unassisted by legal counsel; emotionally, John Doe would have been exhausted after the first trip to Knoxville. But Rocky and Leon were not regular fellas. They approached the court with the likes of a high powered storm. A perusal of their paper trail is mind bending. Even paralyzing:

The court system, governmentally supported and precisely honed by the United States Constitution (particularly The Bill of Rights) is a staid inspiring document. Seldom do individuals with limited knowledge spend their time in constitutional argument. And most people would assume that without standing before the court by a practicing lawyer they would be assured a road to disaster.

A "look see" at the twelve purported Houston grievances unravels information that cannot and did not support their complaints. Passing the bar with a law school diploma in hand might give a person a break, but not much of one. Newly certified law participants would not take the challenge as casually as these men who do not have qualifications or degrees. Not even lawyers duly equipped with expertise, talent and experience would attempt to "sack" the court.

Determining the development of a criminal mind is a worthy pursuit for those who believe steps may one day eliminate crime. Without support from outside, it is doubtful the Houstons would have arduously entered the legal arena. But, according to those who knew them well, "those boys" had plenty of confidence in themselves and no confidence in lawyers. They had huge, exposed personalities. They didn't need that much encouragement to whip up trouble.

With this in mind, pro se Rocky Joe and Clifford Leon presented their theories to august courtrooms. Nothing ever stopped them from going back for more. The twelve pleadings filed during the three years prior to their capital crimes and one immediately after from jail confirms their anti-government addiction. Adamantly, the U.S. Court denied the reach of each claim, which intrinsically carried a reoccurring tall tales theme.

The facts that work against them speak in their paper work: Their unschooled attempts at constitutional rights appear to have been borrowed from someone else's generalized weak arguments. Perhaps similar thoughts traveled underground. No legal footwork gets their theories off the ground. Nothing links sound minds to their incredible propagandized, but empty charges: public corruption, conspiracy, and mail fraud. They do not provide clear and convincing evidence as "proof" to support their off-the-wall claims.

Nothing can bring more lost hope and anger than one's falling into a pothole of his own returning contaminated mental juices. From home, they spray painted their personalized way of thinking like graffiti on their unique legal products; but, their efforts only lead back to black holes: For example nothing connects either United States Attorney General John Ashcroft or the next United States Attorney General Alberto Gonzales to a nationwide conspiracy to take the Houston lives and the lives of their family members. Simply put: they could not connect the dots because they had no dots.

Convincing critical thinking or definitive facts to support accusations are not there. Here are a dozen of those lawsuits to digest and consider:

Chapter 19

The Law Unhinged

Example #1

June 17, 2002 Lawsuit

June 17, 2002, Rocky J. Houston sends forth the first of these selected lawsuits; and, in so doing, he unveils information about himself. The complaint reveals the persona of Rocky Joe, the not so young man. By June of that year, he was 42-years-old and unemployed. Within this complaint he initiates this four-year look at how he mixes half-truths and no truth with vengeance.

For a short while Attorney James Harris of Nashville represents him in this lawsuit. Soon Rocky fires Harris, which through the years becomes an acknowledged strange habit of firing lawyers. So comes "pro se" Rocky:

The June accusations are leveled against those who stand in the Houston's criminal path. Received at 2:30 p.m. at the U.S. Courthouse on Market Street in Knoxville, Rocky's document, in his self-assigned plaintiff's role, names the City of Harriman, Harriman Police Chief Jack Stockton, and "unknown" number of City of Kingston defendants.

An average sleuth can look back at the 2001 behavior referenced within this same lawsuit and hit upon glaring clues. His seeds of abnormal irritation explode here. To intercept Rocky's anguish— glaringly childlike— is paramount. Few humans could keep this degree of anger for so long.

The material he presents in this first example includes what he believes evidentiary material against two municipalities and the police chief of one.

He writes that his privacy and his right to free speech have been violated under the First Amendment of the U.S. Constitution. Historically, courtroom threats and talking out of order are not covered under the amendment. In *Brandenburg v. Ohio* the court said such freedom could be restricted if it was likely to incite imminent lawless order. Such Houston lawlessness was not new to the City of Harriman or to those in the city's small traffic court. But it was reported there that day. Importantly, years of such Houston harangues continued anyway. Of the two brothers, Rocky excelled at noise pollution generally recognized as "contempt of court."

He complains within #1 that Chief Stockton and "two others" in Kingston cost him his job when they sent a letter in 2001 to Wackenhut Security, his employer in Oak Ridge. The letter, according to Rocky's complaint, describes his uncontrolled public behavior. Stockton believed he was required by law to report the incident. Government around the world agrees with restricting "free speech" when behavior threatens. In truth, it is Rocky who is responsible for presenting this condemning picture of himself.

Actually, Stockton boldly stands by that condemnation: The police chief makes an early, accurate assessment of Houston. In Chief Stockton's letter he writes, "Mr. Houston is a walking time bomb," and questions his mental "stability." Jack Stockton deserves credit for his act. Looking back, he was the point man who bravely acted to protect his community.

In #1 Rocky describes how he erupted into what others would describe a violent courtroom tantrum after Harriman City Judge Charles Crass denied his bizarre request for a jury trial to accompany his traffic citation. Witnesses cite a threat that they heard him make against the judge and his family. All of this evolved because Rocky was in court after being cited for speeding in a school zone.

Rocky presents this event in his complaint to the court as it went down, describing his peculiar, frightening, and totally unreasonable behavior. He goes far beyond the law's standard measure for a reasonable man. In this same text, he calls attention to himself by reciting his crazy behavior back to the "feds" to think about:

Yelling and throwing himself to the floor in a writhing fit of anger within the small Harriman court, he says that he begs to be taken to jail. He yells again at the officers to go ahead and cuff him with, "I know the routine." This, according to those close enough to hear, included threats against Judge Crass. Most people would hurry to bury such evidence. Most people would not want to remember a grown up tantrum, nor would they want to assign it to a public diary. Not Rocky Houston. No matter how ludicrous his behavior, he seeks others to blame.

Oddly, he offers up this hot-headed behavior in this lawsuit example. He suggests Knoxville's upper tier of the United States court system see this as innocent behavior. On the face of it, those present during his Harriman fit are not accused of pulling his nails or extracting his teeth to elicit his unsound actions. Yet, he chooses to slander himself as he narrates and continues the memory of this explosive outburst—just bizarre unless produced for Comedy Central.

Of course snickers about Rocky's romp were personally passed around, mainly by the local bar. These lawyers had bent over backwards in order not to offend the mean country boys. And sometimes looking like Houston puppets as they sashayed to the left and right of the pair, the local attorneys needed a bit of comic relief.

How could anyone blame the lawyers? "No! It couldn't be;" and "yes, the man went crazy over a traffic ticket." If the FOX cable program "Cops," had had it as a video clip the segment undeniably would have returned high national entertainment ratings.

Now remember, the federal law community hears this reported fragile behavior straight from the source: Rocky's own June lawsuit. Customarily he complained to news outlets when things didn't go his way. He definitely was high on publicity, which always was as personally negative in nature as it was here.

Then, in # 1 Rocky goes on to complain about the sequence of the outcome: Harriman Police Chief Stockton reports this abhorrent behavior; Wackenhut, serving at the behest of the United States Department of Energy, acts; Rocky's employer requires him to be evaluated by a psychiatrist.

Further, he then passes his mental health evaluation. Within the lawsuit marked #1 for purposes of this explanation, Rocky is pleased to announce his clean mental slate to the federal court. He cites his assigned psychiatrist report: Dr. Ben Bursten writes that he finds "no illness or mental condition which causes, or may cause a significant defect in [Rocky's] judgment or reliability." Well, that opinion and others to follow seem to eliminate an insanity defense to homicide. He also had decided to throw himself on the floor and bark like a dog because he chose to do so. Perhaps way back the psychiatrist knew best. Psychiatrists, perhaps better than others, know that most criminal behavior cannot be easily pitched under a mental illness umbrella. But, how far the behavior of the unreasonable man and his poor judgment will take him will have to be put on hold for a few years.

At his work place in Oak Ridge, according to those who also worked there and prefer the safety of anonymity, Rocky could superficially appear charming and polite. Others there knew a volatile man who quickly turned to a threatening one. A couple such people say he pulled his gun on them. But again Dr. Bursten had it right: Rocky knew what he was doing when he acted. His ego centric nature never seemed to question the direction he took. Lay people describe him as a bit squirrelly. What was the court to think when it read his treatises?

In the end Rocky would be judged as a man who knew right from wrong, who was not crazy when he rushed into the road to kill two men. In this lawsuit, like the others that follow, he always believed he was right.

Most of what he includes here points directly back to his own indefinable spin on the world. His arguments are repetitive and support his belligerence against almost everyone that undressed his dark side, or steps forward to turn down his over heated personality. So it is that Rocky's behavior obliges his critics: He ratchets up his own criminal profile right within the complaint to the court.

Again, this written complaint directly registers arguments that address the violation of Houston's civil rights. He claims his right to due process of the law has been violated as provided under the 14th Amendment. Not many people want to sit over coffee and talk constitutional law with him. Claiming this doesn't make it so. Maybe he is just lonely for conversation.

But, apparently, he takes real pride in his knowledge and believes the federal judges will welcome, even admire, his personal interpretation. And by the way, he always asks for punitive and compensatory damages. That's how it is done.

On June 17 he demands $7 million dollars for pain and suffering and another $500,000 thousand dollars in punitive damages.

At the end of the day, his conceit and ambition doesn't work for him: He accused those who accused him; obstinately he noted his inability to get a jury trial for his school zone traffic citation; he delivered the dramatics of his courtroom temper fit; and then he complained that the Harriman Police Chief, the City of Harriman, and the City of Kingston violated his free speech and his right to privacy. Then, as is often the case, he explains that he hired and fired his lawyer.

Ultimately, the federal court understood the founding fathers' better than Roane County's Rocky Houston. All of this got him nothing; unless he believed otherwise.

Chapter 20

The Uncompromising Duo

Example #2

September 23, 2002

On September 23, 2002 the second in this series of lawsuits bounds forward. Fixed within are the often seen monotonous complaints of the two uncompromising men. Rocky, by nature conversationally high strung, files the second of the twelve complaints. He seems the leader, the one who chooses Leon's direction for him. Inherently his self-righteous need to be recognized perpetuates their ongoing direction.

As the duo confronts all levels of government, they become their own worst enemies. Without hesitation, the aging Ten Mile men continue to take their down-home government mutiny to Court. They might as well have marked their calendars with "This action will be the beginning of their end."

Rocky Joe's "pro se" advances also mark this legal piece and poor judgment. But beneath the surface he gets some help, at least in his document preparation. Each piece of paper submitted to the higher court is clearly formatted, and for the most part presents some required legerdemain. Even experience! Time and effort are obvious. So who might be this silent partner(s)? In one court hearing he talks about his "team." Just who that might be stretches the imagination.

While this anonymous person(s) labors at home in an attempt to settle Houston scores, most Tennesseans think only about University of Tennessee football scores, up the road a piece in Neyland stadium.

If there is outside legal help it might be "on line" via the internet. Law firms do provide advice on payment of a fee. There is small evidence of such downloaded information from a Washington D.C. online lawyer within #2. It, like so much of the extraneous paper, is buried in a rash of other attached clippings and examples. But, with this exception and only small typographical errors here and there, the written assistance seems closer to home.

Houston's own hand on the final page says more: It is shaky and intense. No one can miss the document's accelerated direction: By September 23, his defendant list has grown to six: Scott McCluen, Roane County District Attorney; Frank Harvey, Assistant District Attorney; Jason Legg, Tennessee Bureau of Investigation Agent; Eugene Eblen, Criminal Court Judge; Russell Simmons, Circuit Court Judge; and Angela Randolph, Circuit and Criminal Court Clerk. Then, Houston names numerous others as non-defendants, but co-conspirators: Crossville Attorney Howard Upchurch; Rhea General Sessions Judge James McKenzie; attorney Herbert Moncier; attorney Deborah Graham; and Supreme Court Judge F. Drowota, III.

These sundry chosen co-conspirators, although not included in the suit, pop up in their cited evidentiary examples. The helter skelter complaint also asks the Drowota court to consider the brothers claims of "retaliation, excessive force, extortion, intimidation, and harassment."

Foolishly the brothers push Leon's gripe that they believe the law "manufactured marijuana on him" in a 1993 arrest and unfairly saw a 1994 automobile insurance fraud claim against him. Touting Leon's own past criminal acts just does not make much sense. It certainly doesn't add anything positive to his conspiracy theories. Instead the only evidence here casts suspicion on Leon's forwarded past criminal record.

And while they provide no evidence in either #1 or #2 for these multiple grievances, they gleefully attack people who would not recognize them by name or description. In due time that will change: Those brutally worn Houston faces will be widely recognized.

The same ol' same ol' Houston confrontations continue to assert deprivation of their constitutional rights under the 1st and 14th amendments (#'s 1&2) with the addition of the 6th and 7th as well (#2). As always they thread conspiracy to the charges. The nuisance complaint becomes wearisome as well as those to follow. And they seem but dreary annoyances which in fact precede the Houstons' ultimate solution lying in wait.

"Jointly and severally," Rocky and Leon ask $3 million dollars for pain and suffering here and a measly $500,000 dollars for malicious acts against them. Giving this piece his signature style, Rocky scratches "jury demand" on the complaint's closing page.

In theory, the continued war against the legal establishment unveils a striking social/cultural war which pits the somewhat powerless against the more powerful. Possibly feeling less and less part of the changing community, the Houstons perceive the classical yoke of government coming down hard on their specific cultural class. In this case such a gulf could be identified. If so, a number of people beyond the Houston family also could have felt isolated and powerless. And possibly this is where the men develop their loyal constituency.

Most recently some citizens South of the River had been left behind by a burgeoning crop of high toned city dwellers. The newcomers had built both expensive permanent and vacation homes there on Roane's lake front properties. Multiple people were bothered, but not aggressively so. Assessing the community's past and the fierce loyalties to their own small "neck of the woods" rightly could have taken its toll. Growing up poor carried some pride. Many even saw it as character building. But pride most often dissolved South of the River thanks to the kindred spirits of Rocky and Leon. Disadvantage gnawed. For certain the chosen two opened a breach of dissatisfaction that could have spoken to their growing audience.

Fighting back may have been on more than a few minds. Newer activists with newer ideas came forth at district meetings. School populations and services were sure to change with rapidly increasing newcomers.

The powerless theories are only that. Cheap at best, and reserved for classroom debates, the self-styled insurgent brothers could have been nettled a bit with such academic theory. If so, only other criminally minded people could have sympathized with such hatred.

According to those who say they knew, the bad boy behavior brought into #2 lawsuit began early: In their words, Leon, just out of high school, became known as a "doper," carrying that moniker right up to his alleged capital crimes. Some believe his nickname "Crash" might have been attached to the early drug behavior. Those same people acknowledged that his reputation grew to have "bad ass" attached to it. For a fact, it was whispered; and plenty of people kept out of his way. So while silent, residents South of the River kept their distance when they could from Clifford Leon Houston as well as his little brother. But the silent citizens never missed the tyrants' boiling-over arrogance. Good country people suspected that their whining and widely touted lawsuits had to be "hogwash."

Posting their unschooled arguments to the federal court only had value to those who hadn't read them. And who had time for them anyway? Their lawsuits read at the court level remained mostly unread in Roane County, leaving people there with no idea of what they wrote and no idea of their inferior value. This lack of direct transparency left the uninitiated Houston readers—whether friends or foes— believing that the threatening men had become "big shots" in Knoxville.

Chapter 21

Dead Set to Outlast Court

Example #3

January 10, 2003

Another year of the Houstons' federal lawsuits begins on January 10, 2003. In due order United States District Court's Chief Justice F. Drowota, III makes the Houston's A-list again, with Rocky suing him for mail fraud; the plaintiff, Rocky Joe Houston, returns pro se ; and Rocky Joe throws out a scribbled "jury demand" on the document's final page.

Judges sit to rule, and often to rule the unruly; but the nagging nature of the Houston complaints echo a personal and frenzied abyss. Anyone taxed with their challenges might wish there could be closure. Since it is the purpose of the court to be challenged, the Houston absurd accusations to the higher court truly pose a conundrum: How can the meaningless be explained with meaning?

Evidently, there was no cooling off time between the two-and-a-half months that divide complaint #2 and complaint #3. Full of himself, angry Rocky Joe presses on within the pages:

Beyond Judge Drowota, he adds the State of Tennessee and Tennessee's 10th Judicial Criminal Court Judge R. Steven Babb as defendants.

Recusation leaps forward. In this January piece he extends his anger to 9th Judicial District Criminal Court Judge E. Eugene Eblen "for failing to recuse" (disqualify) himself in an action. Actually, Mr. Houston knows that Eblen complied with the recusal request, but, according to this lawsuit, believes the paper work "never filed" has kept him from getting a neutral, non-biased judge. Studies of such anti-government tactics make this trick a cliché. The recusal ruse has been used by so many anti-government confederates. Here again the lawsuit shows how the brooding brothers seek to break the back of the law in hopes of making the law.

Somewhere there has to be a smirk or sinister smile on the malcontent Rocky's harried face. For him, the old tactic is a measure of his cunning. Difficult as it may be to believe, each time Rocky Joe sees his way clear with fabricated reasons to recuse a judge or prosecutor or ancillary lawyer, he tastes enough meaningful success to continue. In the light of the maneuvers, this becomes a "battered attorneys" syndrome. Over time, he has temporarily held more than one court in abeyance with the ploy. Capturing such moments has to amuse the brothers Houston. And although for now he buys time with his procedures, the best is yet to come: Following the killings, the state will have to search the Tennessee court scene to find a prosecutor, lawyers, and a judge for the Houstons' "murder one" trial. The entire Roane County Bar has been sued or recused by him. Meanwhile, his long term personal demons boil into bedlam:

Lawsuit #3 accuses the United States Post Office of mail fraud and conspiracy—another ridiculous unsupported leap. And, what else? Of course he believes his rights have been violated under the 4th (Search and Seizure), 5th (Due Process) and 14th (Civil Rights) amendments to the United States Constitution. The narrative is repetitively livid with fury, and empty of truth. None of this is what reasonable people would have supported if they had known and could have stopped these men. Right here, and under a microscope, their aggression looks fatefully dangerous.

Speculation arises as the Houston brothers continue their lawsuits. Even with practiced legal expertise of their own, not one paralegal or legal assistant interviewed would feel confident suing anyone pro se. Each sees the practice as brazenly foolhardy. In fact, they comment in agreement that they never would think of doing it. To go without an attorney to the United States District Court would be ridiculous: They would have to be "carried there shamefaced." So what gives the Houstons such unusual arrogance?

Is there a "Book for Dummies" to serve such a purpose? Notably, other anti-government groups have taken up the recusal sport. But, no one looking into the Houstons' conduct has come forth to expose internet messages, phone records, or trips to connect with other concurring radicals. So, if they shared the recusal practice with other groups, there is no evidence. Such other groups have committed homicides in their attempts to prove their sovereign citizen stands. Still no such details connect the Houstons to copycat motives. Their unemployment and last lawsuits do contribute to their tumultuous isolation and irrationality, as in "idleness is the devil's workshop."

Here is the cause and effect: With time weighing heavily on their minds, they believe that they have enemy conspirators everywhere. Not only does their self-styled paranoia sustain itself, it pitches to its highest level. To prove this, Rocky now scribbles a message on the concluding page of complaint # 3 that he "fears for his life and the lives of his family members." No question a lot of fear is being passed around. Neighbors fear the Houstons. The law fears the Houstons. Outsiders fear the Houstons. The Houstons fear far ranging groups of people. Putting this fear on paper is just a cagy way to offer the court a premeditated defense for murder. Writing this continuing message could be a preemptive move. The killer's defense could be: "I thought he was reaching for a gun;" I knew "they were coming after me;" and "I was just defending myself." Nothing new there in the world of criminal defense. Criminals plot. They think they can outsmart their adversaries.

The Houston reputation outside of the lawsuits grew as well. According to witnesses, people scattered when they saw Rock and Leon coming. Sound-minded folks seemed to know something was lying in wait. They got out of the way and waited for it to pass.

The court system recognized the difficulty of addressing what had become infamous men. Those legal minds who answered their incoming lawsuits (as required) definitely would have joined others to avoid them publicly. They recognized maniacal hot air when they read it. And they didn't need the printed flyers put up in the Roane County Courthouse to keep them alert.

The Houston faces were familiar to those who had to deal with them. They had been the subjects of their own anarchist hype, which was carried via both the broadcast and print media. Not one person wanted the kiss of death put on him/her as in due course it would be launched at the two in the Roane County patrol car.

The majority opinion held that these guys were frighteningly both unpredictable and predictable. Expecting solutions became more and more difficult. Since at least 2001, Rocky Houston and his sidekick brother Leon each had worked themselves into a lather. Over time they proved to be less than acceptable human beings.

A few who came forward to explain said this extreme behavior was just an extension of their youthful paranoia. Upgraded by rambling lawsuits, Rocky and Leon exported their troublesome accusations to others susceptible enough to deny major events such as any human being ever touching foot on the moon.

Of course, the Bill of Rights has enormous appeal to both those who stand by its contents and to those who misread it. That is the healthy nature of the nation's democracy. Men like the brothers Houston can wreak havoc with inalienable rights. The justice system quickly tears down such frenzied misconceptions. That is the intent of the pristine document. It gives structure which eradicates the bad and acknowledges the extent of personal freedoms. No where does the Bill give raw, thick-headed intimidators the freedom to usurp the freedom of others. This means that threats and violence and lawbreaking have to be stopped. Go along with what I believe or do; or, if you don't, I may have to kill you. Such behavior or talk obviously would be usurping such rights.

Historically and presently, thousands of dissident and malevolent voices chant, shout or often misunderstand such rights; but other thinking thousands step forward with legitimate complaints against those who they believe have violated these rights. The United States of America is known for such freedom and to most citizens progressively stands solid on the documents integrity.

Not to be missed again here, Rocky demands $1 million dollars for compensatory damages and $5 million dollars for punitive damages. Perhaps the Houstons' anger also went forward as large monetary rewards were denied them. Then again, perhaps such outlandish results could have encouraged them in the way a successful bank robbery can trigger the thieves to rob again.

Chapter 22

Premeditation before the Court

Example # 4

February 21, 2003

Rocky Joe Houston, "pro se," follows eleven days later on February 21, 2003, to represent himself to the Knoxville district of the federal court system. So, without counsel, the court document reads Rocky Houston versus three defendants: the State of Tennessee, State Supreme Court Chief Justice, F. Drowota III, and Fifth Judicial District Circuit Court Judge D. Kelly Thomas. All defendants are named in their "official capacity." Rocky presents a rather miserly four pages. This alone distinguishes #4 from his other lawsuits.

Naming themselves, throughout myriad approaches to this court, the Houstons dwell on their claim they are victims of civil rights violations. Only the list of defendants serves up some variation: Rocky adds Judge Kelly Thomas of Maryville, Blount County. The court dutifully processes Rocky's fixations.

The boys to men remain fixed here on their "constitutional rights" and "conspiracy to violate those rights." Perchance Rocky and Leon harbor a latent student interest in the bookish nature of legal work. If so, not one person asked recalls any such academic insight into the twosome. If early in their lives they had possessed a vim and vigor for legal education it misfired over and beyond them. No one in their immediate environment ever recognized it or pointed back to it.

This February complaint drives their claim that Chief Justice Drowota, along with and Judge Thomas, committed "fraud, wire fraud, and mail fraud" against them. Come on now! Look closely and notice just who is harassing whom. They continue as the self-promoting accusers with restive minds—but not good minds.

The complaints filed in Knoxville continue to award someone's clerical effort. From 2002 to 2006 a nameless someone goes from a fairly accurate typist to skilled word processor. Some laborious soul must have done this out of love. Or, figuratively this person was "under the gun" to get the work done. Even a computer can be a fairly accurate assault weapon put in the right hands. Some dedicated hands kept producing the court complaints.

The spotlight on these twelve complaints should not and does not weaken the earlier years of peddling opinions throughout the local, state, and federal court system. That effort alone would age one quickly. For a fact, the Houstons sent a metaphoric firestorm of such confetti down upon multiple courts.

The continuous complaints between '02 and '06 unveil the grim reality of unruly minds and bodies: Without the law of the land and those who serve it, good people would not be safe. These untamable boys became untamable men.

A search to uncover dark motives continues to manifest itself in Rocky's repeated handwritten adjustment at the end of his complaints: "Plaintiff fears for his life due to conspiracy." The more it is written (usually by hand), the stronger reason to believe Rocky Joe Houston slyly continues to draft a defense to premeditated murder.

In the endgame, the Houstons do not fear dragons! They did not kill anyone named in this lawsuit either. No, they killed a war veteran turned deputy and his physically challenged ride-along companion who had been felled earlier by a stroke. Apparently their alleged crime was a crime of opportunity that allowed them to have their way and live beyond their action. And then....

Leon on Rocky's Heels
Example #5
February 21, 2003

Ten minutes later, Leon's lawsuit enters the court's log: February 21, 2003. The two synchronized complaints lend meaning only to the authors. And are there really two authors, or is Rocky appearing as "ghost writer" for his older brother? No one could label this erratic lawsuit valuable. A right jab, left jab, comes with it, but preserves no connected meaning.

Numbers do add up here: 26 pages and 23 defendants. The acting Attorney General of the United States John Ashcroft tops the list. Similarly accused are 22 other men, which include State of Tennessee officials and judges, notable Knoxville attorneys, and Leon's own past attorney, W. Holt Smith of Madisonville.

Not forgetting close-to-home families and professionals either, Leon sues Pat Cooley and the Cooley, Cooley, and Agee Law Firm, as well as Tennessee Farmers Mutual Insurance Company's Kingston office.

Lashing out at anyone who tells them "no" comes through as expected by now. Leon remembers Judge Dale Young, Tennessee Circuit Court Judge in Maryville, for his admonishing remarks. The judge sternly warned them against their raucous, free-willed courtroom behavior. They claimed intimidation. No surprise of course. They know all about intimidation. Like playground bullies they themselves have practiced it for years.

Then, as often seen within the Complaints, Rocky (or Leon) inserts personal handwritten comments in black ink: "…further more Judge Dale Young told all parties not to involve the court clerk or her office." By now every judge knows how the Houstons like to torment courthouse employees. Although noble of Judge Young, his remarks do not stop them. They link Catherine Quest, that particular court clerk, to the grand conspiracy.

Again the document ends with "plaintiff fears for his life due to conspiracy." Only these two men know whether they expose their paranoia this way, or intend to plant a defense to premeditated murder. But, the Houstons' "fear for their lives" would give insight to a criminologist. The language is tied to the men's recurring behavior. Killing or being killed presents their linguistic identity: They talk about killing often. There was always more to their behavior than surface meaning.

On paper the Houstons' lawsuits throw out a trail of meaningless gobble-de-gook. Yet, these attacks seem to temporarily satiate Rocky's and Leon's desire to be seen as sufferers. Conceivably their investment in time to prepare the lawsuits delayed their graduation to murder.

Crime solving professionals acknowledge that crime and criminals evolve. The Houstons did. The duo profiled their "Waterloo" on paper and publicly. Although professional hands were tied, the justice system's larger community knew a nightmare was lying in wait as a ticking clock counted down on the threshold of their lives.

Chapter 23

Halfway There

May 13, 2003

Lawsuit #6

Rocky, without counsel, moves on May 13, 2003 to "show the court" his next choice of defendants: District Attorney General of Roane County Scott McCluen; Roane County Assistant District Attorney Frank Harvey; Roane County Assistant District Attorney Elizabeth Irving; Roane County Circuit Court Clerk Angela Randolph; Blount County Circuit Court Judge D. Kelly Thomas; and Senior Counsel of the Tennessee Civil Rights and Claims Division Martha A. Campbell.

Here comes plaintiff Houston again, head strong as usual. He wants recusals and wants the court to believe all of the defendants have victimized Leon and him. This behavior has become part of his modus operandi: Kick the attorneys and yell foul! He maintains each defendant named has conspired intentionally and maliciously against him. He also states that the court has "obstructed justice" by refusing to acknowledge Rocky's perceived "conflicts" between lawyers that should force them to recuse themselves. Whatever that "conflict" so close to his heart might have been, he would have done better to look less "conflicted" on the face of things. Rocky, it continues to appear, never listened to anyone but himself. Headstrong "bad boys" seem never to do that.

For a man who tells others how he hates lawyers, he does seem savvy when eliminating lists of area attorneys. In part two of his plan he names them as witnesses (or defendants) in his defense strategies; thereby he asks for their recusal and cites them as part of the conspiracy saga. The legal community was never meant to waste hours sidestepping his maneuvers. And presumably, without available information from splinter groups advocating similar tactics, none of this would have surfaced at all. Definitely not in Roane County. Yes, the idea that such professionals must recuse themselves started with other splinter groups of anti-government dissidents, not with the Houstons. They work the idea here over and over.

His contentious nature evolves quickly into an invective against the court system, and to anyone who knows anyone. The youthful origins of such conspiracy theories, remembered "way back" by his acquaintances, float on the brothers Houstons' sea of mental misery. They stated then and now that conspirators were and are "out to get them."

The threshold of this wish list ascends to $5 five million dollars for punitive damages and $1 million dollars for compensatory relief.

Perpetual Motion
Example #7
July 9, 2003

Somehow Rocky's metaphoric poison pen writes more and more like a dull pencil. Rocky continues to ask for high dollars in damages. Those conspiratorial damages weigh empty. But his committed thinking vexes him to go on. Nothing seems to pacify his action. Certainly he mistakes the court system for the Tennessee Lottery.

The defendants include another most wanted list, some new and some not so new: the Roane County Sheriff's Department; Roane County Sheriff David Haggard; Roane Sheriff's officer Chris Underwood; Roane Sheriff's investigator John French; Roane Circuit Court Clerk Angela Randolph; Blount Circuit Court Judge D. Kelly Thomas; Attorney Herbert S. Moncier; and Attorney Debra Graham. All the defendants are sued for conspiring to violate plaintiff Houston's rights.

As a review of these lawsuits leading to May 11, 2006 materializes, facts emerge:

First, Rocky's unorthodox about town casual wear did exist. In this lawsuit, he complains about the Roane officers confiscated one such bullet proof vest when they arrested him and took him to jail. He complains about not getting it back. So, he did have at least one armored vest. And all that talk about the Houstons fetish for body armor rings true. Maybe there was more. Maybe that is why Rocky left the scene with only a hip wound. Of course it is said the entire ensemble included a camouflage accompaniment.

Looking like parade dressed militia members could have been the behavior of wannabe militia members or just a show of intent. Of course such evidence points to the possibility that they also could have been members of a larger militant militia group.

Then the conspiracy question arises here in #7. Were not the Houstons the real conspirators? By definition a conspiracy needs to include only two people who plan to promote or facilitate a crime. Every suggestion within this and other legal complaints points away from the Houston defendants and back to the twosome who has modeled recognizable conspiratorial behavior.

Next, according to material within Rocky's complaint of the July 9th, supporters of the two men meet July 7th at Clyde Houston's home. So be it: there is a meeting, and the brother's expand their scrap. They assemble "Juanita Houston, Debbie Cofer, Carol Robinette, and John Ray Burnum" "to interview" and "tape record" visiting Roane investigator John French. This meeting seemed to involve Rocky's all too often failure to appear in court.

In April attorney Herbert Moncier, by motion, asks Judge Thomas for permission to withdraw from Rocky's "failure to appear" in Blount County. The motion is granted. Exhausted, possibly embarrassed, he must have had enough of Houston rule. It is commonly known that they believed they knew more than any attorney. Almost any attempt to leave the Houston clients behind would make sense.

Actually, Moncier earlier had provided a gentlemen's "out" for Rocky's recalcitrant failure to appear in court. He told the judge that Rocky was "of the opinion that you were not required to appear before a court out of Roane County."

Thanks to Moncier's kind explanation, the court absolved Rocky of this "no show." No additional warrants were written that day. Obviously, pro-se court participant Rocky selected what part of the law he wanted to understand.

In what appears to be another kind gesture explained in the information attached to this lawsuit, Judge Thomas re-scheduled the court appearance for June 17, 2003 in Roane County. Rocky, being Rocky, resists the kindness and sues the Judge who accommodates him. Talk about harassment. Rocky thrives on pulling off these mean, loutish assaults on the justice system. If involved with other anarchists, he should win the "best of the best" award from them.

Round and round it goes and where it stops nobody knows—yet. But another fact is included in the complaint of July 9: Moncier sends a letter to Ten Mile months later. He asks Rocky, or "your father" to pay an outstanding bill immediately. Proof enters here that Clyde Houston, for years a favorite in the district that once elected him to the county council, repeatedly stands in Rocky's corner. Painfully, other possibilities insert themselves into the father's circumstances. It could be that he is just a compassionate loyal dad; or it could be that he privately fears his sons as others do.

In this court complaint Rocky Joe often slanders himself by providing examples of his bad behavior. He proudly promotes his own ugly actions. But as he builds the case against himself he goes on here to deny that he threatened and harassed Oak Ridge attorney Debra Graham in her private office. He accuses her of things that don't stick and denies the reason she gave for calling the police to protect her from him. The perpetual self-styled defenses swiftly become rancid pudding.

Rocky leaves only one surprise on the table: After all of this Rocky does not show up for his deferred June 17 court date.

Chapter 24

More than Law Geeks

Break for a Breather

Generally put: nobody is above the law. The online dictionary Wikipedia describes the truth of that law is "based on fundament principles and not an act of will." Importantly, that rule is "hostile to both dictatorship and anarchy." For centuries moral men have operated within that law. Not many Americans would want to change it. The phrase applies to all Americans not just "law geeks."

To know the lawsuits is to understand the Houston brothers who willfully believed they should and could take it to the government and win. Their personal anarchy travels the distance of their lives and the twelve included lawsuits. The law gives sued parties rebuttal time in the form of "answers." The written procedure here casts a spotlight on the Houstons' intent.

Democracy gives choices: Whether it be country folks or city folks, people either abide by the law, change it, or break it. Separatist, aspiring to self-government, actively break the law. They desire to eliminate the code of the civilized world—not just here, but elsewhere on the globe. The men from Houston Hollow knew that route.

Evidently, when questioned by followers, the Houston two convincingly explained that they were saving the country from conspirators who were destroying America. There are layers of enforcement to stop insurgents such as Rocky and Leon. But stopping them takes each and every layer's cooperation. Within the cooperation, consistent controls and courageous hearts mean everything. Passing along the depth of what might happen to the public is nearly impossible. Physical threats and the possible loss of life can grow quickly and silently.

For example, the Houstons had the building blocks of home rule in place. They had secured boundaries right down to the public roads adjacent to their property. Although privatizing a public road is against the law, men with guns can do it on the spot. Standing against those fellows seemed out of the question. Yes, according to reliable sources, people who were stopped on Barnard Narrows just turned around and left.

Insurgents want no part of the rule of law. And those left standing against them should not only be law geeks—or the bookish minds that poke around law libraries. It seems that their recusal tactics and failures to appear in court should have ended way back.

By August 14, 2003, Rocky Joe sent forth the paper work to subpoena Judge D. Kelly Thomas to appear in the United States District Courthouse. As with multiple others he commands the judge to appear; he plays with what he wants to destroy, much as he did when he attempted to handcuff Judge Russell Simmons. He believes this should force Judge Thomas to excuse himself from Rocky's court appearance. Fat chance that he can get this past Thomas. But his faithful get a different message. They must see him as United States Supreme Court material, or at least governor of some state—albeit his own. They allegorically are ready to nominate him. They believe in his abilities. The brothers Houston for years on end mesmerize that audience. Reversing the rule of law means nothing to people with emotional loyalties and perceived but unaccountable grievances.

Brazenly, the Houstons "catch me if you can" attitude prevails. Rocky continues to harass with his incomplete and unmerited subpoena forms. As always he uses dictatorial emotional combat as a trade for his empty academic standing. Similar headstrong tendencies most often surface in young children. They seldom linger to adulthood as they do here.

Unfortunately part of the wider audience considered this behavior a comedy for too long. No wonder: In the television series "Andy of Mayberry" character Ernest T. Bass seems to fit that label some people applied to Rocky (and Leon). His creators portrayed Ernest T. as a "wild man from the mountains" who brought raucous laughter when he chose a lifestyle in conflict with Mayberry citizens. He was also known as a nut. Ernest T. was generally a nuisance who committed petty crimes for attention. Perhaps those who originally overlooked the Houstons' behavior considered "Clyde's boys" no more than a nuisance.

Evidently in Rocky J.'s case, his nuisance-styled, attention-getting lawsuits went further from the outset. Roane County's Houston was dead serious. Mistaken as entertainingly foolish, his reckless obsession with the justice system needed to be brought to a close. Known as a trained government sharpshooter who could be bad to the bone, he somehow claimed self-defense in the alleged murders of two men.

A Houston Highlight
August 18, 2003
Lawsuit #8

In a little over a year's span (June 17, 2002 through Oct. 27. 2003), the Houstons will send eight law suits to the Federal Court.

Plaintiff Rocky Houston primarily continues his complaints against six defendants in August: Roane County Circuit Court Clerk Angela Randolph, Circuit Court Judge D. Kelly Thomas, Roane County District Attorney General Scott McCluen, Roane Sheriff David Haggard, Roane County Sheriff's Investigator Randy Scarborough, and Assistant District Attorney Frank Harvey.

In addition he assigns negative star power to three others: Tennessee's Governor Phil Bredesen, the State of Tennessee, and the City of Maryville. Mastermind or mindless, the man recognizes a few new accusations will spice up his personal applause meter. Here he may reap an ovation for attacking the Governor. Bredesen had done his job when he helped both Blount and Roane counties to bring Rocky Houston in without bloodshed. After earlier unsuccessful attempts to deal with this man who continued to resist state law, the Governor acknowledged the need to stop the behavior. For that Rocky and Leon sue him.

By now it is Blount County authorities who contact his Oak Ridge employer at the Y-12 nuclear plant. They follow in the earlier footsteps of the Harriman police chief who reported to Y-12 in 2001 that Rocky was a "walking time bomb."

Wakenhut the security contractor and Mr. Houston's employer asks him to promise his that he will show up in court on the earlier warrant, and gives him a somewhat temporary reinstatement. He doesn't! As any Houston follower might predict, Rocky decides to quicken the pace.

In this case it becomes the quickening pace of his heart. Stricken, he chooses Oak Ridge Hospital Emergency Room to the Courtroom. Leon calls in his "chest pains" to the court where he is due to appear that day. Whether Rocky borrows some psychological manipulations from Joel Chandler Harris' thinking character Brer Rabbit or not, ER Dr. John Mesner runs customary tests and clears him to leave. Houston remarks that he "feels fine" now. Health restored, the vituperative Houston again has failed to appear.

Mr. Houston's tomfoolery makes both Blount and Roane Counties emerge pathetic, and Tennessee's governor gets sued. Without blinking an eye, one might guess the storyline here: Rocky's legendary path borrows from not one but two childhood characters. Think *Brer Rabbit* outthinking *Brer Fox*; or choose *The Boy Who Called Wolf*. Regardless of choice, it is kid stuff. Appearing in court might cause some people to have a heart attack, but coincidences are seldom coincidences, and seldom are they in the context of his usual behavior.

Wisely, and in hindsight, Sheriff Haggard kindly allows the Kingston Police to send officer Brian Mullis, a Houston acquaintance, and Paul Lloyd, the Shiloh Baptist Church Pastor, into Rocky's Barnard Narrows home to bring him in on the outstanding warrant. There Rocky concedes to them and leaves. Of course, all the while, he knows his second choice is a standoff with a state Special Operations SWAT team. The SWAT leader takes him to jail. Mullis rides with them.

The law's plan works—that time! But Mr. Houston's coveted "Q clearance" with the Department of Energy is gone for good when he goes back on his promise to turn himself in. Why yes, the United States holds to the rules under the law. The guy went willingly, as it was explained later, forgets the additional force that was going to take him to jail if he didn't go.

Either due to sincere fear, gripping paranoia, or outright falsehood, the plaintiff Houston sues nine defendants in his August 18th complaint with conspiracy to commit murder, false arrest, false imprisonment, slander, defamation of character, conspiracy to intimidate by excessive and deadly force, invasion of privacy, conspiracy to interfere with the plaintiff's livelihood and the plaintiff's family, and conspiracy to interfere with the plaintiff Houston's business relationship with Oak Ridge Wackenhut Securities, as well as interfering with that Department of Energy's coveted "Q clearance," which he chucked.

Then he puts his final touches on his repeated perceived civil rights violations: Constitutionally he points to the 1st, 4th, 5th, 6th, 7th, 8th, and 14th amendments.

Yelling foul whenever confronted by law enforcement is a standard practice of multiple criminal types. Specifically, Rocky Houston's busy mind explains the world the way he wants to see it. An unhealthy habit for certain. With false confidence, he continues to slide down a dark harmful slope. Evidently, at least according to the Sheriff, the only loved one who attempted to trim back his painful direction was his mother. With his mother gone by

May 11, 2006, there seems no one who could hold him back from his willful destructive personality.

Behind the government security badge Rocky was "the man." Rocky's psychological need for acceptance and a public identity seems flex- tied to his alleged May 11th slaughter and crime. The heart of his matter and a revealing trail of evidence are kept secure on the stacks of paper sent to the court. This August complaint is again typical of his calculable footprints. Understandably, his loss can loosely be described as identity theft: He now complains that he has been without a badge for two years. The implication within is that Wackenhut Securities filched that identity when he had to give up his job and those coveted credentials. He does not admit to refusing to follow their instructions to him on his outstanding warrant.

The bleakness of rejection can cut a bit of a man's testosterone swagger. Textbook theory often links some male criminal behavior to the excess of that hormone. Officially at least, he could no longer be recognized as a man hired to carry a gun. Blaming someone else for yet another loss in his inventory of losses seems right to him. He sues wrongfully.

Wackenhut, founded in 1954 by George R. Wackenhut and three other ex-FBI agents, began as Special Agent Investigators. With the original name packing a punch, the corporation's business (now a division of Group 4 Securicor) grew and is the second largest security firm in the world. Impressive. The company's Oak Ridge contract rests with its ability to guard the Department of Energy's nuclear facilities there. In turn they must promise a vigilant management of their employees. In the end, the job of guarding such facilities equates to guarding the country, and importantly guarding all of its citizens.

Now wearing a badge can blow a man's ego way out of proportion. Pump him up a bit with power. So, losing the right to wear that badge, as well as the paydays that come with it, can leave a crater inside a fired fifteen-year-veteran like Rocky Houston. Perks beyond retirement might have included a complimentary recommendation from the company when employment ends; the history of an admired government security clearance; the right to go armed on the job; and, without a doubt, one's self-esteem. Such accumulated loss has to be noticed. It goes to the core of a person's well-being. In this case, the loss seems to have brought on more than he or anyone else wanted. But no person of integrity could continue to overlook his confrontational acceleration and personal decline.

Within this particular legal complaint, Houston unveils more than his usual rant and rage. Rocky J. Houston again comes forward "without counsel." Here he goes beyond the suit of his former employer for firing him to include Wackenhut's Director of Protective Services, Steve Gibbs, once his boss. Questions circle: Did Rocky not understand his job description, or the government entity for whom he worked? Or, was it the Department of Energy's Wakenhut who did not understand who they had hired to work for them?

Lo be it to the employer who stands behind the law as Wakenhut did. If anything, the content of this lawsuit (#8) portrays a man miffed for ever being served a warrant. Somehow he doesn't understand or like any part of it.

Dog-eared "warrants" must mark the Houston law dictionary. Rocky's life turns on warrants. He decides to mitigate the official service process. Personally he must see it tit for tat: he set about serving subpoenas against those who want him brought in on such warrants. Control is everything. Warrants turn him inside out; the subpoena process must make him feel boldly better.

As he attempts to defend himself in the August 18 lawsuit, he instead incriminates himself with his usual long winded fumes: For example, Rocky proudly recalls signing a warrant for the arrest of Roane Circuit Judge Russell E. Simmons, Jr. He does not address the rest of the story where it is alleged by witnesses that he attempts to handcuff the upstanding, affable judge. Perhaps once again it would be understood better if it was fiction.

Without hesitation the "Andy of Mayberry's" Ernst T. could pull off a laugh with that behavior. Factually, it is called "contempt of court." In court, such farcical behavior can escalate quickly. The law understands. One is found "in contempt" for showing disrespect for the judge, disrespect for the proceedings, and disruption for the courtroom.

Disruption is what the man is about. It is almost a personal diagnosis; significantly it is also a diagnosis of thinking attached to common law court cultists. His behavior copies the identical published behavior of such anti-government groups when he assaults the judge with handcuffs. Yes. That too has been done before.

Behind that Wackenhut security badge he once wore, hidden envy may have lurked. Rocky's distaste for lawyers is there; but he wants to act like a lawyer. He worked as a security guard but spoke openly of "having to kill a few cops." He pushed an anti-government agenda, but had a father who had become an elected official.

Perhaps the badge was never enough, and his hatreds spewed forth from underlying jealousy. Turned differently, such unhappiness might have motivated both brothers toward an ultimate happiness. Both men's aggressively determined nature could have become something other than what it did.

In retrospect, the brothers Houston' worst enemy was not the government but themselves.

Chapter 25

Court Moves

October 27, 2003

Lawsuit #9

October 27, 2003 marks the entrance of plaintiff Rocky Houston's pro se argument against D. Kelly Thomas Jr., Blount County Circuit Judge, Maryville, Tennessee; Mark E. Stephens, District Public Defender, Knoxville, Tennessee; and the State of Tennessee.

At first glance, the complaint looks less than lethal. Then he talks about the then U.S. Attorney General John Ashcroft who conspires against him, and also complains (that's right) about pubic defender Mark Stephens— the guy who just wanted to help him out. Then old Rocky works himself up to speed. He gets out his usual tape recorder. He wants to keep the unlucky Attorney Stephens straight. Good will doesn't go far here with the Houstons.

Now he revisits his multiple suits against Judge Kelly Thomas for nothing more than knowing the people with whom he works ("having a working relationship with…") as assigned to the judge by his position in the court system. Right away, Mr. Houston's rancorous thinking is ramroded across the turbulent essay to include citing the judge for not acknowledging Houston's attempts to subpoena him. PLEASE! Talk of not playing well with others.

Seeing the world through Rocky Joe Houston's mind takes commitment and patience. Within that mind, his ego driven authority circumvents all other authority. His need to topple such authority figures drives his life. He fortifies his opinions with charged anger and lists—lots of lists. Subpoena lists. Defendant lists. In a real world there would be outside distractions to relieve him of his self-inflicted stress. He marches on.

Houston's lawsuit history casts a net over government and government officials. How those empty nets proceed for years speaks of his unrelated but never explained personal angst. Only Charles Dickens' complexities in *Bleak House* might shed light on something similar: the characters in his novel spend years and years in court on a torturous unrewarding trip through 19th Century England's legal system. The only reward is that it finally ends, but badly. Death instead of success grips the contentious participants in the end. The novel's broad analogy shows the far-reaching, damaging consequences that failed legal disputes can bring to those who die captured in their own orchestrated misery.

Houston's piece of art here references Clifford Leon's troubles: Older brother Leon sees John Ashcroft as a personal nemesis. Then, the lawsuit names Blount Judge William Dale Young, perhaps not a comparable to Ashcroft, but here joins Young to the United States Attorney General's conspiracy against the men of Barnard Narrows Rd. How so many people find truth in the Houston behavior is baffling. The question takes a hold on reasonable minds. Geographic loyalty must have given the Houston circle blind faith in the brothers Houston.

Clearly, Rocky becomes more dedicated than most petty criminals at attracting attention and gaining notoriety. He makes himself a legend in his own time. Moving his name to Knoxville in his federally directed paper products heightens his notoriety. He is a hard dude to forget. Too, who wouldn't remember a man who after helping him comes at you in a lawsuit with both fists? For certain, both brothers created enough strife to keep their storyline alive.

This October 27th complaint (#9) gives an inside look at an October 6th posse gathering on 373 Barnard Narrows. This meeting place is a pace or two west of where Jones and Brown died. Leon's home is at 412 Barnard Narrows—the family home place and scene of the shooting.

Somehow impossible to visualize, Rocky's house has a dual purpose. It is both a place to talk anti-government politics and a home to Rocky and his wife. It is also the domicile for their two teenage children. Most of their visitors live close by and are related.

At this early October meeting there, Rocky says he tape recorded Mark Stephens, 6th Judicial District Public Defender, supposedly an invited guest at the get-together. R.J. Houston goes on in his lawsuit to describe what sounds more like an interrogation room with rocking chairs, than an "invite." Clyde Houston, Leon Houston, and Rocky join together to participate in this closed-door interview of the public defender. Gary Parker is also a guest there.

The agenda blasts Stephens. He, according to Rocky's lawsuit has been wrongly chosen by Judge D. Kelly Thomas to defend Rocky. He "improperly picked him by telephone" says the man sitting there with this crew. No kidding, Rocky believes this is an aggravating circumstance. He wants to nail Thomas for providing him with a guy to help him in trial preparation. Somewhere in between these thoughts, the Houstons' invite Stephens into Houston Hollow. The target Stephens must immediately know when entering the place that he never should have made the turn off Highway 58 onto Barnard Narrows Road. How such an appointment could have Rocky and family riled so is inconceivable. Oh that's right, Stephens must be conspiring against him for the judge. And everyone knows the Houstons believe all kinds of off-the-wall conspiracy theories. Isn't anyone there a bit embarrassed about the way Stephens is treated? All so strange for a law suit.

The repetitious fabric of the Houston arguments must have caused true consternation within the justice system. But perhaps those at the Barnard Narrows meeting believed Rocky was the Pied Piper. Advisedly, old friendships and kinship shouldn't go that far. The Houston set probably didn't know how to say no.

As a matter of fact, other pieces of the lawsuit remain unperceivable: Rocky Houston uses his plaintiff's lawsuit to call up some of his own past bad behavior. He points to the Harriman Court episode, where his threatening conduct and "Waco" threat combined to be declared a Class E Felony for "retaliation of a past act." At the time, both in state and in federal court, he realizes the legal services of Roane Attorney Chris Cawood, Knoxville Attorney Herbert Moncier, Oak Ridge Attorney Debra Graham, and Nashville Attorney James Harris. All seem to have been only short time Houston associates.

The lawsuit characteristically spins on. Droning on might be more descriptive. His conspirators have violated his constitutional rights, according to his interpretation of the 4th, 5th, 6th, 7th, 8th, and 14th Amendments, and he sees his financial stakes heighten. Within he asks for combined damages of $10 million dollars. Could this bewildering additional need join to others to set him in motion for murder? Perhaps a $10 million dollar gift would have fixed everything. Perhaps he truly believed he would be so compensated.

His "respectively submitted" signature, although an expected formality here, opens another window into the man's troubles. Respecting polite society has its day in court and out of court. Most often it does not extend to a child's view of respect which ends with the "yes ma'am or no sir" from the inherited culture of small children in the southern United States.

But those children grow to learn more. As men and women they decide to curb their anger in order to save themselves and others. Such other adults think through the end results of contemplated bad acts and decide against them: Ultimately action and reaction rebound back to a fellow. "Mo bad" will catch you every time.

Chapter 26

Serial Drama

February 13, 2004

Lawsuit # 10

Another season begins in the serial drama of Houston and Houston on February 13, 2004. Unusual, although it has happened before, it is Leon instead of Rocky who files his pro se complaint. Perhaps the somewhat more than three quiet months of down time since October 27 of 2003 left the two without stimulation. Then too, idleness can be tempting.

Leon lists fourteen defendants. Most of Roane County residents have held to a flawed belief that the Houstons only fought with local government. But that is far from the truth. The contentious "aping" of real lawsuits tells a different story. They attack larger government on impulse, and they do that often. Routinely the State of Tennessee is a defendant as is the Tennessee Bureau of Investigation or someone employed there.

Senior partner Clifford Leon sends forth the February complaint, but junior partner Rocky Joe leaves his forensic language all over it. Of course, if one brother is there the other brother is not far away. Maybe it is Leon in spite of the sameness. Maybe nothing says that brothers cannot have a genetic writing style. Even so, the tract assuredly mimics Rocky's well-known prose.

Part and parcel, redundancy is impossible to miss here, whether it is Leon's effort or Rocky's design: Leon believes seven of his civil rights have been violated. Then, as a matter of course, Leon contends that the law has done him wrong. The Ten Mile two do not acknowledge that the law, according to peaceful citizens, helpfully restrains the improprieties of wrong doers. Of course, they always blame others for what they do criminally.

Their continuing, unrestricted pro-se arguments directed at constitutional minds can mean trouble—trouble for almost anyone who is not educated to tackle the material. They certainly are not! Just the required complex set of civilized readings, laws, or procedures would deter most people. A regular guy would be quick to recognize that he is without those talents or abilities, and he would back off. He would follow by either hiring someone who knows the legal landscape and procedures, or he would stay out of the fight. Fortunately most people recognize the face of superiority when looking up at it. They listen and learn. Not the Houstons. They never conclude that their bluster doesn't make the grade.

Their inability to control the courts may be what ignites the finale of deadly fireworks. Conceivably, when they find themselves emasculated by their failed court attempts, they seek refuge in a different kind of fire power. Their arsenal of weapons noticeably has given them a more comforting control over such goals.

Many sources close to their story say the brothers have lived intimately with their weapons for years. In fact, neighbors, business people, and fellow Y-12 employees provide accounts where the men talked up and displayed their guns in front of them. Without a doubt they knew their weapons. Without a doubt they knew how to use them.

Rocky's profession required the knowledge of firearms. They never tried to conceal that fact. And according to their past history with law enforcement, Rocky, at least at one time, had a concealed carry permit. Most people who have the right to carry a concealed weapon never run afoul of the law, never shoot anyone, never brandish them in public, or even display them on their person: In fact, keeping weapons "concealed" is the favored code of behavior.

Rocky and Leon did not abide by this protocol. People saw it. People feared it. Some who never reported it to authorities saw Rocky make threatening gestures with his gun. Yet, it was their unstable personalities that frightened people the most. Smart people feared the mix of the habitual volatility and the guns.

With $400 dollars spent here and $500 hundred dollars spent there to carry out their lawsuits—at the post office counter, for service of faux subpoenas, or for filing costs—money added up. The nature of the spending asks inquiry. Such choices could not fit into most peoples' budgets. Stats show Rocky and Leon continuing to spend this kind of money on their court harassment. Expensive anger!

Reasonably the court must be shown material evidence and justifiable reasons to serve subpoenas. Seldom does anyone, even if he believes himself a pro se plaintiff, miss that point. The Houstons' liked subpoenaing small names and big names.

But without factual evidence it does not pass muster. Common law or Houston law, many would be able to recognize it as government harassment. Tactically, it pushes aside the United States' rule of law, the rule of peaceful men, and just the old fashioned rule of decency. The evidentiary failure is paramount in each Complaint. Simply, a Houston belief system does not support the truth. They need relevant facts to support the truth.

More factually, things never cool down; and the Houston men, even while sitting behind bars, never cool down. While they await trial for over two years they yell, they accuse, and they file lawsuits. Allegedly, a scheme to break out by one of them is discovered and prevented.

During this period where it must be assumed that Clyde Houston spent the customary high price to hire lawyers to represent them, the brothers remained inflexible and unhappy. Law breakers pay a high price for high crimes. Wasting a defense lawyer's time with your contorted opinions seldom brings a rewarding outcome. And screaming out against attorneys, judges, and John Doe citizens just doesn't work the same when one is behind bars. Regrettably, in the past, a gun's cocked hammer can work pretty well. The Houstons were comfortable with that possibility. Time and again, long before the alleged murders, local officials had to beef up the safety of the courtroom and even the courthouse when the Houstons arrived. Many beyond law enforcement fretted about what lay in wait. They did not want the repeated violent nature of these brothers to provoke a brew-ha-ha or worse in a secure community building.

Within lawsuit #10 neighboring Blount County's Judge Thomas's January 13, 2004 order attempted to prevent this possibility. He tells court officials not to allow Leon into the courtroom during a scheduled proceeding involving his brother. The same thing happened in Kingston where Chief Jim Washam took similar measures to protect the integrity of a small municipal court. They both recognized the brothers' combined lethal emotions and feared for the safety of others. Of course the team Houston held contemptuous feelings for anyone who proceeded against them.

The Bible warns against being your brother's keeper. To serve one's brother totally seemed each man's choice. However their tight bond never takes on a religious or humane explanation. Their contemporaries' expectations for hearth and home, church instruction, community, entertainment, work, and sports would not have allowed fanaticism to fell them or their families. Those following the Houston lead were a different ilk.

Chapter 27

Red Flags to Red Flares

July 8, 2005

Lawsuit #11

The Houstons' July epistle marks significant 2005 calendar events. Within ten months and a couple days of their last Complaint, the brothers Houston allegedly will launch the shootings from the vicinity of their porch. Red flags turn to red flares for Houston watchers: In these accusations sent to Knoxville's U.S. District Court, Rocky shouts out his torment against 66 defendants, which definitely speaks of burgeoning numbers. Rocky's spiel points to this angst and supports what some believe to be an indication of his galloping paranoia.

Immediately he boldly announces that he, in fact, is the direct recipient of "domestic terrorism." Twisting the phraseology, his use of words reveals the continuing nature of the slick or the sick brothers grim.

Whether a true insurgent himself, or man believing he is a wordsmith, Clyde's youngest son acts most often like a bad tempered child. Surely, it is the "anti-government" brothers here who most clearly fit the general explanation for "domestic terrorists." And although Rocky craftily reverses the terminology, he does so illogically. His lawsuits follow no more of a logical route than his shouted tirades. Working hard here in #11 to convince the court, he seems to fail. Reading the ill-connected thoughts unveil both superficial and silly exposition.

His argument accuses United States Federal Judge Ronnie E. Greer of a "direct and intentional act of domestic terrorism" against the Houstons. Then he prays that United States Attorney General Alberto Gonzales focus on "… the domestic terrorism by the above mentioned defendants and come home to America." If there is anything here that makes sense, someone within the anti-government thinking would have to translate it. Is he telling Gonzales that homes along Barnard Narrows should set the standard of all Americans? Again, these isolated few seem to elect themselves to lead the nation.

The large game in Rocky's attack here in July of '05 against multiple defendants goes beyond the then U.S. Attorney Gonzales to include six federal judges, Tennessee Governor Phil Bredesen (again), Roane County's own Deputy Governor David Cooley, and the Federal Bureau of Investigations' Beth O'Brian.

His belief in America's conspiratorial stand against him is tantamount to all that ails Rocky Joe Houston. For the twelfth time he characterizes a chain of evidence against his multiple unproven enemies. One example is his characterization of a pretrial conference before Federal Judge Curtis L. Collier. He tells the judge to recuse himself because "you have been named—been subpoenaed as a witness for— this man here— to testify in an upcoming case…" Then, raising the whimsy of his personal threat level, he asks for private protection for himself and his family in a manically shrewd aside. As if there to educate the judge in this matter, he goes on: "We got U.S. Marshals." The meaning interpreted suggests that the judge should send more government lawmen to deal with his authored suspicions. "We" of course means to him that the judge and he have the same standing in "their" choice of decisions. Unless he is auditioning for the Cartoon Network, "this man here" continues to angrily show his "in your face" audacity.

Brer Fox hardly conceals Brer Bad. Unquestionably, the Eastern District of the United States Court (or any court) cannot and should not have to deal with Rocky or Leon Houston (again unrepresented by counsel) whose mental boundaries entail continuous frenzied minds. Those who are hired to preserve the peace have a similar problem trying to contain the Ten Mile two's behavior.

When citizens cannot appreciate or support those who must take on these huge responsibilities, they are like birds putting their heads under their wings, believing bad behavior goes away. Looming problems never do. Band-aid remedies are temporary. Most choices mean helplessly waiting for what's coming. With the courts and law enforcement watching, the rest of the community had little choice but to wait for the violent threat to escalate into more. They recognized the havoc and saw it for what it had become: a longstanding and continuing nightmare lying in wait.

Many of the people in their South of the [Tennessee] River community for years had acknowledged their intractable temperaments. If "hell" is a place of ungodly chaos, as described by theologians, then one developed there below Kingston where plenty of good people had no choice but to live with it. Un-timed but lingering, would be the hellacious anti-government shoot'em up of the brothers Houston.

Message from Jail
August 27, 2006
Lawsuit #12

Oh yes. This lawsuit comes from a lockup—hardly the last either, but the last lawsuit to gel the nature of the nightmare. As often reminded, a serious analyst knows that it is not over until it is over. Filing accusations or "Complaints" never really stops following these shooting deaths. For that matter, although this focus ends on the last of twelve complaints (2002-2006), the document is just the last to be included here. Complaints continued while the Houstons were incarcerated for over the two years they awaited trail. This Houston document accuses three defendants.

One of Rocky's named defendants and South of the River neighbor, Roane Sheriff's Deputy Faye Hall would soon be dead herself. Returning to her home, she was killed in a traffic accident on Highway 58. Before she died Faye had been forthcoming with her opinions about the Houstons and remained steadfast for her boss Sheriff David Haggard; she did not live to go forward at trial as a prosecution witness.

With Rocky in jail, Rocky's wife, Nancy C. Houston, files the suit. She names herself power of attorney for Rocky. Without a seal or stamp, which customarily makes such a document official, she proceeds. When the Houstons talk "family," they mean it in a DNA kind of way. If you are blood kin, you had better carry your weight in loyalty. Nancy's marriage to this man demands that loyalty as provided here in the twelfth lawsuit. With the Houston name and Houston children, she is linked to the whole.

The two other defendants in August are the United States Postmaster General John E. Potter and Roane County Sheriff David Haggard. Haggard, within months of the shooting and this lawsuit, comes close to death himself. It is reported that during a required surgery he has a heart attack.

Yet, health problems take no visible toll on Rocky and Leon. News photos show them to appear as healthy as ever. Rocky, particularly, is looking good.

Contributing his ebullient mood for the press, he gives thumbs up gestures, throws kisses, and steals the camera's eye with each manacled trip to court. This man never hesitates to work his way with the justice system. By now, the Houstons and their vocal supporters are sending out a strident volley of self-defense theories as the brothers Houstons' motive in the homicides.

In Rocky's message from jail, he says "the Sheriff's Department of Roane County conspired on May 11, 2006 (that infamous day) to create an impediment" to delay the filing of this very same federal complaint. Simply put: The two dead men died by getting in his way and interrupting his work schedule. He is afflicted by his lawsuit's delay, not by the death of two men, nor by his incarceration. It is unclear whether Mr. Houston is referencing the impediment in order to implement his developing homicide defense; who knows. But he definitely says that law enforcement brought this final obstacle to his doorstep in order to stop his legal rifts with the federal government. He must mean that he knew this could happen, and when he perceived it as such he would bring the behavior to an end.

Even behind bars, he portrays the incident that holds him there as a mere speed bump. Think about it. In the end, the grand conspiracy messed up and forced him to delay "the filing of this Federal Complaint." Labeling Jones and Browns as hindrances is the equivalent to removing pylons used to re-route traffic.

Evidently with this "impediment" literally put to rest, Rocky Joe continues his war. With only a few of the Houstons' "conspirators" dead (Jones, Brown, and Hall) what will happen to those other named conspirators they have been miffed with over the years? Could this ultimately mean more could die? Or will others just get letters from jail?

The focused texts of these selected chronological court complaints end here; but repeated numbers of written Complaints, according to public record, continued to arrive in Knoxville. Then just months prior to the schedule July 14th trial (ultimately in two separate trials) for the brothers' two counts of first-degree, and an additional felony murder charge, Rocky's life as a "pro se" attorney and conspiracy theorist ends.

The U.S. Court for the District Court of the Eastern District of Tennessee says Rocky is prohibited from filing more of the same conspiracy complaints. Enough is enough.

Chapter 28

Straight Answers

"Vague, conclusory, obtuse, and absurd" were repeatedly used as the Houston accusations were answered over the twelve months explored here. In the judicial process a plaintiff(s) (here that of either Houston brother) files a Complaint(s) and the defendant(s) answers. The Answers may also contain affirmative defenses. They must show a denial of all the plaintiff's allegations which the defendant(s) wishes to challenge. Obviously this is usually the work of lawyers. Obviously, the Houston plaintiff(s) is not a lawyer. When no facts or evidence support the plaintiff's lawsuits, the process reaches a dead end, but calls for a description of the situation. Long explanations that included the quoted adjectives in the first sentence above (and a tome of others) build the Answers to the Ten Mile documents.

Anyone who might pity the innocence of the poorly educated can stop right there. Each time the Houston duo sent a legal Complaint, they received copies of the instructive Answers. They had time to read and reread how and why the rules and the laws went against their all consuming self- possessed meaningless declarations. But over and over and over again Clyde's boys repeated the same behavior. Metaphorically, they redundantly sent their failed essays uncorrected back to the teacher. Of course they never looked for instruction. Evidence adds to the paper harassment goal of similar minded cult groups across America: The Houstons set out to encumber the court with Complaint after Complaint. To them, dropping a claim in a red, white and blue box marked for U.S. mail could be likened to putting a "three" through the "hoop" at a championship basketball game. Explicitly, a few examples below of "answers," sent to the Houstons can save tired eyes:

1. The Houstons continued to ask defendants to recuse themselves when they were told particular recusals were not legal: "Clerks have absolute immunity for quasi judicial functions. As an elected official a clerk cannot recuse himself/herself as a clerk in someone's case."

2. The Houstons, so it would appear, both purposely and routinely filed the exact lawsuits multiple times: The plaintiff "has sued multiple individuals and multiple courts over the same event." And, "the present case is filed for the purpose of **harassment** and needless increase in the cost of litigation."

3. According to "42 United States Code 1983, the case must be pleaded with some degree of specificity." Nothing new here: Complaints were sent with no supported or supportable claims.

4. A lawsuit against their "elbow counsel," a lawyer provided for them without cost so that they might "better navigate through the system" tells a lot about their intentions and who they were: They earnestly set out to bring despair on the United States justice system and individuals within it.

Although the list could go on and on, citizens might better understand these selected few answers taken from the large number of replies, which also include:

5. By injecting the federal court system into his on-going criminal matter, the plaintiff is attempting to hinder the proper procedures in state criminal court by subjecting officers and employees of the state legal system to frivolous time consuming and costly lawsuits at every turn. Plaintiff is using his federal court lawsuits as a sword in an effort to recuse judges, obstruct the legal process and thwart any attempts to hold plaintiff accountable in his own on-going criminal matters.

6. Then in reference to sustain law in Stump v. Sparkman, It is a judge's duty to decide all cases within his jurisdiction that are brought before him, including controversial cases that arouse the most intense feelings in the litigants. His errors may be corrected on appeal, but he should not have to fear that unsatisfied litigants may hound him with litigation charging malice or corruption. Imposing such a burden on judges would contribute not to principled and fearless decision-making but to intimidation.

In all cases, no amount of explanation could loosen these law breakers bonds to meddling with the law. And even when more and more anti-government cults went "under," or just underground, the Houstons could not see the end of the road—even though their ultimate game had been set aside by others.

But, a bit of the fervent anarchists' instruction known best to the country in the 90's was something that attached itself to the brothers and to their not-too-original schemes. The brothers found an underlying need to carry out the court-directed charade.

If they did hold to the Common Law militia approach of the nineties, perhaps it made them whole; perhaps it gave them direction that they lacked. So it goes for people with idle time and nothing to do with it. Ironically, that devil's styled workshop of idleness heatedly worked overtime. Nothing like giving purpose to one's life.

Plenty of people in Roane County substantiated Rocky's and Leon's spoken testimony to such behavior. According to witnesses, they both saw themselves as part of the nationally organized Freemen and the Common Law Court movements. Rocky, in accordance with that particular thinking, said he was going to give up his citizenship but didn't.

The Freemen movement, according to the United States Department of Justice, had "engaged in 'paper terrorism' through much of the 90's." Those organized groups clogged legal and financial institutions with phony documents. They, like their Roane look-a-likes, also threatened government employees. Their ultimate goal was to conduct court proceedings in their own "Common Law courts." Looking back, the Houston's gnawed on an old bone so to speak. Perhaps they were part of a larger group, but were passed the leftovers. Or perhaps they were more connected than anyone cared to prove.

In 1994 the Freeman had offered a bounty of $1 million dollars on individuals who acted as a local prosecutors and or sheriffs. Two years later on June 13, 1996, 16 members surrendered to law enforcement. The Freemen movement supposedly ended then and there. The Montana group had been dismantled by federal, state, and local authorities following a nearly three month armed standoff. Other research would show similar groups still operating secretively.

Another Houston borrowed idea must have been come from a Freemen derivative practice: This was known across the country by federal law enforcement as the Common Law Court movement which was barely masked in Houston behavior: This group "uses the constitution to support their notions of 'sovereign citizenship,' whereby they become immune from federal authority," said United States Justice Department warnings on the subject. This notion looks to have been either plagiarized or practiced by the Roane dissidents. Those who were adverse to the risk of being named in this book tell how the Houston brothers sought to influence or impress others with talk about making themselves sovereign citizens, immune from the law. Both brothers talked openly about it. They were always full of big talk that they did not back up; of course, that was until they admittedly tied themselves to the deaths of two men.

BOOK THREE
Trapped in Themselves

Chapter 29

Déjà vu Teaches

October 8, 2006

By the Fall of 2006, although a somewhat timely distance from that spring's homicides, the unhallowed eve of the deadly event had not gone dormant. Yet predictable picture perfect scenery outlasted the bodies and blood and bad acts. The Smoky Mountain's palette of earth tones had painted over the recent past's stark reality.

The Kelly Green of the Houston pastures stands out in early October. The morning of October 8th began as a mellow one. To me, there had been a long five months between the alleged Houston brothers' crime and the remaining year's calendar days. For me, it was time to go home gain.

But then, I was trapped in my own sentimental time line. Nothing could have convinced me that anything lie in wait for me. I guess if it hasn't happened to you, it hasn't happened.

Living about 400 miles away for twenty years had put my own sometimes conflicted memories on hold. Now, I returned to find enormous joy with the best of friends and settled personal history. Roane County can bring out the Spartan strength in people; it was my time to respectfully acknowledge the gift it had given me.

A friend had agreed to spend this day as my hostess. Rocky's and Leon's gun crimes were out of sight and out of mind. The only shots waiting to be fired were digital ones from the small camera on the seat of the car that I was a visitor in. Roane's "South of the River" setting clearly remained a top notch assignment for a National Geographic photo journalist. My driver, herself born a neighbor to Houston Hollow, masterfully drove along the narrow roads with glowing pride for her community. Unwittingly perhaps, we rode into the valley like giddy schoolgirls.

Finding this old friend with a great laugh helped me relocate my emotions. There was no fear attached to what in the past would be considered a Sunday afternoon drive. But, I had been warned by other friends to be careful visiting anything south of Kingston; and it was foolishly that I disregarded their advice.

At that time, due to my professionally honed literary journalism training and private experience, I wanted an objective "look see" at my past. That plan would have to include a patch of the Houstons' present place on the map. Part of the memory lane that my friend and I wanted to cover included turning from Dogtown Road west on Barnard Narrows, to Highway 58 and then onto Cade Road. Once, I had spent a lot of time there in Cade Road fields and pasture, eventually becoming a part-owner of that property.

As we were about a quarter of the way into our quiet trip, we approached the Houston family homes that abut Dogtown and the general area. In that direction we headed to Barnard Narrows. Distantly, from this approach, the byways of Dogtown and Barnard Narrows meet dead ahead to merge and to connect in a curve. Moving ahead, the most singular admission of the Houston clan's presence was the private cemetery in the grazing land to the right of the car.

I had advocated this trip to make sure I had a glance at the once known Cade farm, now the Cooley farm. I had loved both sides of the ridge, and certainly had liked this circuitous route for getting there. The Cooley and Houston properties had met where cattle and kids approached the long narrow peak of their shared ridge line. The Houstons land then truly was on the other side of the mountain.

Today no cattle wandered up or over the top. Cattle were missing from the Houston fields. Kin were no where to be seen unless one considered those buried in the quaint private cemetery way out into that field. Both the bothersome brothers' mother and aunt recently had been put to rest there. Both Rocky's and Leon's mother and aunt had died in a close proximity of time and lay safely in this peaceful spot just prior the shootings and now. An old wrought iron fence and accompanying shade trees dignified the graveyard like a requiem hymn. At this point, no onlooker could look away from the memory of the 2006 shootings and the year of the Houstons.

The crime hesitated in my mind, because I wanted to remember with fairness the Houston families. I had moved to Roane County when Rocky and Leon were small children. Somewhere within myself, I was pushing my own learning curve. It turned out to be more than a historic one. The lingering sight established a peculiar tranquility. But my personal and professional direction immediately conflicted. How could I divorce the fact that I knew two others had died unnatural deaths right here: Two men whose "lives had been turned over to God" by the hands of others. Tears on the human condition pulsed beneath my selectively protected scenic view. The setting started to spill forth its own story. My camera, acting here and there, clicked along the way.

Not far beyond the intersecting curve ahead lay the exact spot where Deputy Bill Jones and Mike Brown had learned their own final lesson. Believe me, I wasn't thinking about learning mine. We casually moved on. My natural bent to defend underdogs almost anywhere forced me to give the brothers Houston that fair look. Hardheaded, those back roads of my mind had led me astray before to be dead wrong. Yes, I knew I carried a "do gooder" trait or two. "Do good" had even been the motto of the college sorority I had joined. Undone by going too far by such behavior before, I should have quickly counseled with myself about allowing my mind to go there. I wasn't looking for trouble.

And so this piece of my mind became fateful: If knowing about the Houston anarchy was not enough, an unexpected incident soon would teach me better. But all of that hit me head on down the road. Minutes away, and out of nowhere, all of that would change. Suddenly I found myself totally immune to any early sympathy I carried for the Houston circumstances.

At a glance, the poetic house by the side of the road that I remembered as the Houston homestead stood strong. The old two storied home held its historic place with dignity. It looked back to us from the pitch of its high roof line. I hoped it would be so. I wanted to remember the porch apron surrounding the house—the front of it almost in the road— and the forest of tress that had always been there. The scene fortified the house's legacy (quite besmirched now) as well as my remembrance of things past.

A closer look pinched like a painful bright light intruding on my vision. My brain said "close your eyes." I didn't. So, I saw the home's yard riddled with miscellaneous neglected toys and debris (soon to learn left there by Houston followers). Even so, I wanted that picture. I had collected pictures of other Tennessee farmhouses that I wanted to draw and paint. I could eliminate the house's recent distressed appearance with several brush strokes.

Slowing down and almost stopped, we hesitated. No one seemed to be here at what had been Leon's home on May 11 when the alleged first degree murders took place on this spot. Still assuming the position of most civilized people, neither of us felt there was a need to get permission to take a picture from the road. Looking back, but never having gone back, the Houston "pull over" and the road definitely seemed one in the same. No one would think about getting out to measure it. We didn't.

For all appearances there was no one to whom we might wave hello. Then too, my memory attached to Sam Walter Foss's poetic lines of "…let me build my house by the side of the road and be a friend to man." I had chosen the lines in a high school speech competition to give a thesis to my message. Sam Foss and the Houstons had different approaches to visitors:

Once into the curve of Barnard Narrows, we "old girls" unwittingly were tracing the path of the two dead men who had been blasted away with rifle rounds right here in front of this historic setting. Deplete of people, vehicles, or activity, the landscape and the home appeared to be empty. But, perhaps unknowingly, like Deputy Jones and ride-long Brown, we had been marked long before we came to a stop. Did we stop in the road or on what they believed was their turf? There was nothing in concrete to distinguish such a difference. It would take a plaster cast of tire tracks and a team of surveyors to make that distinction. We didn't pull up onto their grass. We must have been on the public road!

We stopped. I remember one digital click of the camera. Suddenly cars dropped from the sky like ghost riders to lock us in place. I still had my camera, but instantly thought about my life. I always will believe since then that Jones and Brown only had moments of thought or reaction time.

According to these faces that must have been relaying our travel for several miles, we needed to get out of there. My friend recognized them as Houstons. There was no recognition between them and me. She jumped out right in the middle of the road to explain who she was and who she had always been. Even though I stayed seated in the car I could feel the threats directed at both of us.

My friend's car door stood open. Then a woman, who ended up being a younger sister to Rocky and Leon, leaned in to me through the door. Checking me out seemed a priority. An attractive woman, looking and sounding herself somewhat like Daisy Dukes of television fame, she questioned me about our being there. She talked and I answered. I tried to keep the conversation genial. I recalled the Houstons as small children, but not these children grown and presumably gone bad, although they were one and the same. In her case, I thought of my own sons who must be close to her age. This recollection took me way back. At this poignant moment in time, we both must have recognized things had changed. I was sixty-five years old, just a year younger than her recently deceased mother. I think that must have been important. But, she startled me with this examination.

I was on high alert. Instantly, I thought in a linear direction to who she was and her devotion to Houston tactics. She definitely prepared me for ugly possibilities. Now, after the fact, I must admit there was something about her I liked: Her grit maybe. Maybe I had learned it the same way.

But trapped here with one of us in the car and the other outside of it, the group had honed in on us as if they were birds of prey. Right then I recognized that indeed there were multiple people who owned that publicized Houston behavior. Neither she nor the others outside of the car had any appreciation for the two detained women. Old they were, but with plenty of grit of their own. Of course age had taught the two of us that this was no place to prove it. And no one would ever figure out if there were guns there.

Interestingly the woman shot out mixed messages about who she liked and who she didn't like. Lawyers and law enforcement personalities were on her "do not like" list. These named people were quite familiar to us both. I wasn't on the good end of that deal.

In the same vein and quickly following, she dropped a sinister bombshell: Right in the midst of the nervous chit chat, she said "Stay out of here—or you will have an accident on this road. The road is dangerous." She said it with a look to kill.

My friend came back to the car simultaneously. We left. I cannot remember exactly when I told her about Debbie Houston's threats to me. Then I looked back. Not safe yet.

More ghost riders were behind us. Without delay these cars followed us out to Highway 58. Apparently those we left behind had practiced their drill before and wanted to permanently barricade the public road. From there we went as planned onto Highway 58 and then Cade Road. Safely on the other side of Houston Hollow, I realized we had relived a little or a lot of the double homicides. The exception here was we lived through our ambush. They didn't.

Healthily transferring my only good memory to a Houston horse who poked his head into the road toward my side of the car, I smiled at his soulful eyes and his polite farewell. I hope they treat that animal better than they do people.

I also pictured horses and their owners in times past trotting up and down Barnard Narrows with some civility. Yet even back then there was criminal behavior and danger. A story on Shoe Boot road just a skip and a hop away speaks of a man and a horse (possibly a mule) who went missing never to be found. A shoe boot was the only evidence ever turned up. So enough about looking backward towards civility and the times; perhaps history is only the repetition of events spelled out differently.

It was on the Barnard Narrows spot right in the tracks of the recently dead men's marked patrol car that my commitment to this book internalized itself: When my pictorial whimsy settled and turned back to unexpected threats against my life, I knew I had a job to do. My curious need to know had turned to knowing. And what I previously might have believed no longer held weight. Believing can stand in the way of fact. I took my facts and ran with them. There was evidence here that I, as an old news hound, knew needed to be told to others.

These alleged double homicides of 2006 pushed me into a riveting two-and-a-half years of research and writing. Although this October experience did not speak directly to the dead men's demise, it brought me closer to those terrible moments.

Unnamed publicly prior to a trial, Debbie Houston's name circulated in rumors as one of those on the porch minutes before the homicides. If incorrect, had other rough but personable women with friendly smiles casually gathered on the porch prior to the patrol being snared? Is this what prompted Jones to turn the car around, believing he might learn more about Rocky's whereabouts since it is also reported Uncle Ray was out front minutes before. So it is believed, an active warrant was out there for Rocky. The possibility that the unseen brother was hiding close to the road, even on that first pass just as these "ghosts" must have been who lighted suddenly on us, will stay with me. And I always will wonder if they had gotten "the word" just before the deputy drove past that he was in route and close to the Houston location. Had someone alerted the men to their soon-to-be approach? Such quick notice worked against my friend and me.

Our incident and their deadly incident were pointedly similar and coincidental. All of those moments in time, as reviewed, proved again how easily one can be ambushed by criminal minds. Investigations prove to be dangerous as well. More than likely, Jones and Brown were returning to the farm house to investigate and inquire about something that they didn't seem right. Was it the missing Rocky?

On October 8, 2006, while separate county jails held the "boys" behind bars, their minions definitely wanted to ratchet it up for them. We were random targets.

Chapter 30

The Waco Manifesto

Rocky Houston at first not different from others who are cited for traffic violations wasn't happy about his 2001 traffic ticket, but showed up in court. The late 19th Century building housing the City of Harriman's Offices and traffic court has a significant history. It is still known as the Temperance Building. Those who combined religion and alcohol abstinence built their building and movement there in 1891. A few years later it became the home of the American Temperance University. Nationally they successfully raised a significant number of others to crusade against the sale of alcohol. In fact the temperance movement won that war when the proposed 18th Amendment was ratified in 1917. It took effect in 1920 and was not repealed until 1933. The 21st Amendment reversed it.

Rocky's intemperate behavior in the Temperance Building brings a wee smile. Judge Charles Crass routinely fined him that day for a cited traffic violation. Not exactly road rage, but most clearly traffic ticket rage got the best of him. He insisted he was owed a jury trial.

Then he did it. When he realized he was not to get the trial and had to pay $50 for exceeding a posted school zone's 15 mph limit, he went hog wild. Houston's threatening warning to those there took hold: "if you can remember Waco, then you haven't seen anything yet." No one could have missed what he meant when he recalled the hellish vision of the Waco standoff between the government and David Koresh's followers.

Then and there, Rocky Joe erupted into courtroom behavior that went beyond any reasonable person's expectation. It wasn't pretty. The need for him to ask for such a trial was baffling. First reports described his crazy response with humor. Normal people are not well acquainted with the signs of accelerating criminal behavior.

He went into a tirade, say witnesses there. According to their description, he provided a display of temper even Saturday Night Live audiences would have frowned on. For sure, it was no laughing matter. More than likely his extemporaneous behavior invited the community-at-large to see a bit closer into Rocky Houston's plans and possibilities than he had intended when he exposed his goal. Newsworthy as the man's screwy conduct was, it was his Waco threat that stuck.

Hardly any American alive on April 19 of 1991 could forget "Waco." Most concur that the fiery inferno, which killed 81 people at the Branch Davidian compound in Waco, Texas, should not have happened. Similar thoughts surround who or what at this point in 2001 could have atrophied the Houston crimes of 2006 before they happened. No one accomplished that end or was able to stop their frightening, churlish behavior. The tyrannical two went on to ramrod their behavior across five more years. Clear similarities between the Waco cult and the Roane compound existed then and now. However it was no other than the Houston men who made others catch the clue.

Clearly, Rocky's raging outburst substantiated a wish to ignite a similar tragedy in Roane County. He had a plan up his sleeve and he was to be the "doer." Using the national nightmare to incite fear was bad, real bad. On the face of it, only those who had dealt with him over the years had a glimpse of real trouble yet to come. Lyrically he depicted a true "Rocky road ahead." Quietly and firmly a few citizens who prefer to remain anonymous tried to avoid the man who wanted to kill. In other words he was seizing other people's space and freedom.

His proclaimed threat took up where his logic left off. On the spot he measured his hatred of government by that of Waco's leader Koresh. Koresh, although only having completed the ninth grade, dictated the behavior of those suppliants who sought his counsel. Godlike to some, the Waco leader (as well as the brothers Houston) proved to be just another screwy, controlling human. Mr. Koresh gathered followers much in the manner of the Houstons. Both preached against a government conspiracy set on destroying America. Both instructed others to save America for their children "while there was still time." Such popularized messages by anti-government disciples were tired expressions to scholars of domestic terrorism. Less connected friends of the Houstons believed Rocky and Leon had initiated those phrases and that thinking.

Rocky never had been alone in his cultish Waco beliefs, and he was not alone that day in Harriman. He brought part of his own home grown audience for support. If anyone close to him privately had questioned these fanatic outbursts as signs of a disrupted personality, or faithfully justified it as required oratorical leadership, no one explained. Instead all in his contingent agreed: Rocky was Rocky because he had been "harassed."

The youngest of the co-dependent brothers, Rocky was the most outspoken of the family, creating devotees well beyond his kinfolk. So, with God as his witness, he persistently baited the public and gained supporters with similar attitudes.

From this particular courtroom appearance in 2001, his childish tactics escalated instead of diminished. If one contradicted the man's moves, he or she became the villain. In this most ironic of methods, Rocky used his own bad behavior to upgrade his usual claims of harassment and government conspiracy. Somehow he was successful on blaming his own unseemly bad acts on others. At some level, his juvenile propaganda took hold. The exact nature of that same game was "nothing new under the sun," as the wisdom of the age's passes along: He simply chose loaded messages which appealed to the emotions of his group and eliminated their powers to reason. Rocky did well here selling his persecution.

Believe it or not, in circuit court where Rocky's traffic case bounced after his Waco threats, the threats were denied in a written statement by the traffic court's Judge Crass. Finalizing his 2001 courtroom charade, he added that "we've got some sorry, corrupt people up here," as he threw himself on the floor in the memorable surreal episode. "Up here" could have only been directed at Judge Crass, who later swore that he never heard any of what seemed to have been directed to him and his courtroom. Saying that he didn't hear them seems odd, but perhaps he didn't. With Judge Crass's inability to acknowledge the threat, the reported key evidence could not deliver a guilty Rocky. Instead a Roane County jury ultimately decided to absolve Rocky of the nightmarish outburst. Although other court witnesses substantiated hearing the threats to Crass's courtroom, Houston was forgiven of his reported criminal outburst.

Those who viewed replays of the episode said he even did some hearty barking. Could it be? Then Leon went after a court official with an umbrella when the man stepped forward to take his video camera. And who was that who thought Rocky and Leon should have been bonded out after the killings?

Consequently, due to lack of evidence or a local jury's fear of possible retaliation for going against them, Rocky's penalty was minor. When Rocky got his chance to cool down he didn't. The smart attempt to abort Rocky mania failed. Instead things heated up.

Perhaps this success encouraged his cultish charm. He must have left the courthouse believing that the community would continue to absolve him of any future criminal culpability. Looking back, the constitutional promise for a jury of his peers is a frightening proposal. Those who stood against the government were growing. Many others did not want to vote against anyone in the Houston clan. They were beginning to reluctantly recognize that they might be marked. They wanted to live, and this meant living with the Houston darkness.

Reportedly, some did refuse to serve on his jury and were excused. One man boldly announced that he could not waste his time listening to the reputed craziness that followed the Houstons wherever they went. And crazy it was: even after the trial that absolved him from his outlandish behavior over a traffic fine, Rocky wasn't pleased or relieved. He did not like the jury's decision to charge him with disorderly conduct and another small fine. He left that day predictably unhinged.

But Rocky Joe had a way about him: his characteristic charisma held up. The preposterous self-confidence had hoodwinked people into defending his accusations. And the younger Mr. Houston never ran out of confidence.

Warfare instead of welfare ruled their thinking. Only hallucinatory personalities could hold onto the belief that interconnected layers of United States Government had conspired against them. Domestic terrorist authorities, such as those at the Southern Poverty Law Center in Montgomery, Alabama surly would have labeled the Houstons as plotting, anti-government conspirators. Somehow they had worked under the radar as "local yokels" who had miles to go before they were truly known.

Most individuals change as they mature. The socialization process turns around strident childhood behavior. In the brothers Houston's cases, societal attempts had failed to modify that childhood behavior. Both brothers were in their 40's by 2001. Rocky, reportedly the hottest head of the two, had not changed during childhood, adolescence, or adulthood. In the Temperance Building he asked courtroom officials to bring it on when he knelt and threw his hands behind him begging to be cuffed: "I know the routine," he yelled. Arrogant with confidence, he apparently went looking for a fight he didn't get. He had chosen the wrong bar. Atypical of rabble rousers, Rocky did not choose a bar room scene for notoriety, but chose the esteemed bar of justice.

Rocky eventually got his ultimate jury trial centered in years of publicity, but not the one he demanded on the traffic violation. Having barely completed high school, his lessons to others were substantive: Rocky Joe taught others how to play the system for nearly two decades.

Giving the world that blood bound piece of his mind back then Mr. Houston caused considerable consternation. He knew it would. While crying out his Waco warning and accompanying threat he made his timely statement. Watching a grown man have a public tantrum had to be alarming. Who could deny that it went further? The man melodramatically simply unveiled the truth to do real damage to some or all of those on his long list of enemies. Multiple courts knew those names. He repeatedly had provided them in writing for over more than decade.

Looking back after the alleged 2006 double first degree felony murders his fuming outburst five years before came across as a commitment to the premeditated slaughter. Yes, reasonably the law enforcement cadre who hoped to stop the Houstons didn't. But credit is due for their effort. In their attempt to get him stopped, they may have saved a great number of lives beyond the men he killed.

In retrospect, it had been that nightmare lying in wait. The Waco remark was the Houstons' calling card. But the Waco recollection did not go down in history as did "Remember the Alamo." Both were in what became Texas, but the latter recalled heroism. That memory heralded Davy Crockett and approximately 30 other heroic Tennesseans. Those long remembered volunteers died along side another 190 Americans defending the growing country. Rocky, who wanted his listeners to believe that he could produce something more disturbing than the Waco memory, was only allowing his demons to drive him.

East Tennessee's Rocky Joe and Waco's David Koresh wanted followers to fear them and the government they lived under. Beyond a doubt, Rocky thought well of himself. When speaking in court about himself he acknowledged his own presence with "this har man." In due time the menacing brothers would surly be out of sight and eventually out of mind when they were locked up with others who had carried out deathly goals.

Similarities between Houston anti-government doctrine and Waco were many. The Waco siege was also about long outstanding warrants never served and never accepted; it was about stashing a stockpile of weapons to include Kevlar vests, body armor, and high powered rifles; and history has it that the rumor of Texas's anti-government cult holding semi-auto rifles with a similar enlarged capacity turned out to be true.

A growing number of people had reported the Houstons talking big about their bunker and their arsenal. If any of that was fact, a great deal of money had to have been spent. Whether or not the Roane County men could have accumulated such a secreted armory of weapons over time without the backing of culpable parties, outside financial resources, or networked ideology remains in question.

The leader within the Waco fortress did not go down in history fighting for his country. He did not stand bravely alone in his defiant confrontation with the United States government. Koresh took his followers to their deaths, to include 25 children.

Described before and after as a psychopath by the press, Koresh had for years fortuitously depended on his own twisted survivalist plan. Getting people to die with him and for what he said he believed took unusual charisma. Rocky and Leon Houston had their own following and their own charisma. According to those there at the time of the duel homicides, it was Leon who told others to leave the porch when he believed there was going to be what the military calls a "fire fight." Right then, Rocky comes away looking as a less compassionate guy than his brother.

Chapter 31

Wacky to Waco

Some might see similarities between yelling out threats of "Waco" in a courtroom as similar to shouting "fire" in a crowed theatre (a legal standard for judging free speech limits under the First Amendment). In this case, Rocky just stepped it up a bit. After all, those fiery Waco scenes broadcast across the nation's television screens looked like the "eternal flames." He knew recalling the Branch Davidian deaths would awaken people.

The United States government's decision-making at Waco brought unmistakable shame and somewhat fair allegations against the government's decision to enter the compound. The torrid topic itself ignited a myriad of other timely anti-government cults. Even ordinary American citizens pondered the judgment call which brought such destruction.

So it was that numbers of anti-government types sought reprisal. Whether Rocky and Leon Houston had officially joined others in the treacherous ilk remains in question. Still, the Waco battle cry heard in Harriman in 2001 must have been on Rocky Houston's roadmap for some time. Whether or not he blurted out his threat in the heat of the moment or meant to strategically announce his deathly potential remains uncertain. Rocky was sometimes an impulsive guy, but known for his repetitious agenda. Clearly, his angry shouts highlighted the Ten Mile two's continuing theme.

The Houstons would fall under the brand "militant," but would be more difficult to label as "activists" since that label would be a bit high brow for the brothers. "Activists" are seen most often as forward looking and original.

Original thinkers they were not. But "domestic terrorists," according to literature on the subject, would be a tag suited to their anti-government behavior. Conversely the Houstons branded their named conspirators as "domestic terrorists." For them it was just more childlike tit-for-tat lingo, and definitely that which identified them: You are! No you are! Blame, blame, and more blame.

According to the FBI/ Department of Justice as well as the "Intelligence Report" of the Southern Poverty Law Center, anti-government patriot groups that "roiled the 1990's" had come to a close almost by 2006: At their peak there had been 858 groups nationally. This information points to the execution of Timothy McVeigh as its turning point. Quickly, minds were changed.

Apparently though, according to intelligence made public, some of the more covert "patriots" had moved to an even "harder line" of the radical right. The ebb and flow of those people who support such groups can be described as conspirators, cults, criminals, or crazies. With few exceptions, criminal intent weighs more heavily with them than political theory. The Houston fellows fell right in with the larger group.

People ask why criminals do what they do; the next question is how? The why and how of the Roane brothers' motivation must have been deeply embedded. Perhaps it was not completely known to them.

Behavior scientists look to cause and effect in long term or short term responses. Sometimes combinations of those responses join to exist together. The cause makes something happen and the effect happens as the result of the cause. A bystander's assessment points to scattered causes and effects that could hold some weight have been suggested but not been professionally questioned. The combination of the two speaks more loudly.

Social change or limited opportunity may be culprits that contributed to Rocky's and Leon's fired up angst: Culturally they stood on ebbing local losses. As farm boys they had been parked on the precipice of extinction. If the land that they lived on and would one day inherit had converted to well-placed land for development they already might have turned it to gold. That had happened to many in East Tennessee, but not to them. With neither of those choices, they and other country people had fallen to the bottom of their own agrarian culture class.

On the other hand, if they had considered giving up their family's land to lawyers and legal fees, the thought did not deter them from killing. Their barefaced lack of "emotional intelligence" ruled against sound thinking.

For what ever behavioral reason, the "boys" saw themselves as heroes in their anti-government drama. They never needed to audition for the roles. Over time, acting as their own press agents, they successfully elevated themselves to their headlines—headlines that earned both their oft quoted harassment declarations and others' privately held, but recoiling laughter.

The last laugh seems to have gone to the Houstons, while the chuckling audiences stood back taking a lot for granted. Whatever caused people to see them only as a joke returned with a vengeance. Their growing disruptive nature never should have been abided. Something there was terribly wrong. The sheriff, family, and friends should have seen it much earlier and worked, if they could, to settle them down.

In reference to gains and losses, it would be easy to recall TV's "Beverly Hillbillies." Popular characters Jed and Granny were also caught between cause and effect: country heritage and new money. Even with wealth they were rejected. But their cultural missteps brought laughter not loss.

Here, even if loss was ever part of the Houstons' lives, the effect was anger not laughter. Perhaps Rocky's and Leon's narcissistic bent became their undoing: Never insightful, they could not unravel the emotions that wouldn't let go of them. Instead, their unsanctioned thinking led them to temptation; and, it was that self-serving temptation which led them right to incarceration.

Chapter 32

Sociopaths in Their Own Heroic Story

A textbook approach to the duo's behavior can reveal what many believed they recognized in Rocky and Leon as personality disorders. No psychiatrist or psychologist who dealt directly with them ever saw it that way. Profilers who study sociopaths make such behaviors definable. And in so doing, the literature on the subject describes rogue conduct which extends beyond the average person's interpretation of "wacky."

According to eminent Dr. Robert Hare, expert on sociopathic versus psychopathic personalities, sociopaths **live on the edge, are prone to verbal outbursts, feel contemptuous of those who try to understand them, blame others but never themselves,** and are **superficially charming;** he also adds that they are **authoritarian, glib, without empathy, paranoid, grandiose, tyrannical, and extremely narcissistic.** Most of these qualities add up to self-absorbed human beings. They are good at fooling and convincing others of almost anything, but definitely just as good at passing out pain to those who love them. Such statistics mimic the Houston drama; but, experts emphasize that not all sociopaths kill.

Sociologists and criminologists differentiate between sociopathic personalities and those of psychopaths: They believe sociopathy is a mixture of a genetic predisposition and environmental factors which most often look back at poverty or parental neglect.

Studies claim that a sociopath's desire to **live on the edge**, never winds down. As with other characteristics they exhaust their spouses, parents, and children, who stand helplessly by, or are taken into their mental web. Parts of the South of the River community believed Clyde Houston, the men's father, and their recently deceased mother must have experienced a similar exhaustive pain contingent to their problems. But Clyde was there in the end and he stood by them.

While seismographic warnings went out over Rocky Houston's **verbal outburst** in Harriman's small city courtroom, the buzz held to their observed outrageousness. Again only Harriman Police Chief Jack Stockton, along with two Kingston officials that the brothers Houston were unable to uncover, took notice in 2001 and acted.

Stockton, acquiring those two consenting signatures, sent Rocky's Oak Ridge employer a letter that described their security guard Rocky Joe Houston as a "walking time bomb." And, over time, the Harriman, Kingston, and Rockwood chiefs stood together in attempts to solve the continuing public threats raised by the Houstons. If Stockton and this round table of alert law enforcement professionals had been critics in this "Theatre of the Absurd," they would have been award winners for recognizing the meaning beneath the chaos. The strung-out lawless nightmare had preyed upon Roane citizens, according to most, for more than the recognized fifteen years. Yes, Stockton elected Sheriff following the 2006 ambush killings, called those "shots" five years earlier. He wanted to reign in the danger, but had no idea when and where that figurative "time bomb" might explode. He recognized the depravity but not the time and place. He and Washam both had long identified that nightmare lying in wait.

While "the law" could keep an eye on the brothers, they were not mental health professionals. Textbook mental health treatment, according to such professionals, advises cognitive therapy. None was suggested, and none was forthcoming. Along with the snug fitting profile went a complication: Sociopaths are **contemptuous** of those who try to understand them. And sources who are part of the large extended family divulged, while asking not to be identified, that Rocky's and Leon's instability seemed certain, but no one would have suggested it to anyone else in the family circle. In Appalachia, even a private denunciation of a family member is a cardinal sin.

Looking back, the sociopathic behaviors alerted outsiders too. Doing something about the growing possible outcomes just was not available at home where they would have done the most good. In fairness, perhaps family intimates tried unsuccessfully.

No one should miss the astute behavior of Judge D. Kelly Thomas. The neighboring Loudon County judge was onto them quickly too. By requesting a second psychological workup to follow the one Wackenhut had decreed earlier, Judge Thomas joined the minority who read fear when he witnessed

Rocky's uncontrolled explosive behavior in his courtroom. Of course his foresight did not eliminate him from the "touched" pair's lair. They went on to sue Judge Thomas for taking part in a conspiracy against them. Looking back over their years of photographic headlines, their sociopathic behaviors seem painted across their faces.

By now an additional psychiatrist delivered his findings to the court. And as usual, this report came forth only to decide if the examined subject was mentally capable of standing trial for his alleged crime. Guaranteeing privacy rights, the doctor deemed Rocky competent. He said Houston understood the charges against him and the trial proceeded. If there was more to the report, it was not at that time made public.

Meanwhile, a developing, un-adoring group grew. They did not support the Houstons and believed that the brothers Houston were merely "mean, ignorant rednecks," who believed they were Ten Miles "tall and bullet proof." No doubt silent voices wanted them stopped. They certainly didn't want to die trying. Rightly so, that should be left to law officers.

Judge Thomas must have seen what law enforcement saw: disturbing personalities with the inability to forfeit responsibility for their continuing obstreperous acts. Faulting themselves was unknown to either Houston man. They definitely measured up to the forceful sociopathic tenet of **blaming others for their bad conduct**. Those conspiracy theories and harassment charges must have emanated from internal miseries. As time accumulated over those fifteen plus years (miscellaneous charges going back to 1991), responsible public personalities, asking not to be named, said no proof ever validated the Houston's harassment claims. Of course no one attempted to get the opinion of the two United States Attorney Generals or the President of the United States who had been sued bogusly by the Houstons.

Still the duo's spin encouraged others to believe what they had to say. Disturbingly, the dead men's lives never took on the sympathy that Rocky's and Leon's harassment defense did while awaiting trial for their alleged 2006 homicides. Dead men Jones and Brown were merely put to rest. Of course the state's prosecution had taken up their fight quietly and privately most of the time.

An objective study of the Houston lawsuits unveiled no substantial evidence of harassment. The federal court system substantiated that. The brothers' (most often Rocky's) rife deficit in critical thinking betrayed their own arguments. Reasonable men do not take it upon themselves to subpoena huge numbers of miscellaneous people in one lawsuit without providing an inkling of convincing evidence. Their oft named defendant lists appear to those who have read them as arbitrarily chosen names. Railing against lists of names was certainly hollow of thought. But personally to them, firing such paper off to the court would escalate to firing bullets at living beings. And this acceleration of aberrant anger was documented way too long. The Ten Mile two spoke and acted in the manner of sociopaths or children as they refused to accept blame and continued to blame others.

A thorough read of the Houston lawsuits is laboriously bewildering. Normal people cannot put themselves in those shoes. It drains the kindness from the reader. Good people rely on multiple sources to legally stop such firebrands from their disastrous course. They couldn't. Those who supported this behavior clearly should at least feel ashamed and possibly culpable.

Some people who rode their wave, so to speak, believed them **charming**. Back to recognizing sociopaths, who are particularly captivating for their own purposes. Many people appreciate magnetism in friends, politicians, preachers, and most leaders. Sorting out those who are insincere from those who are sincere is left up to the individual. Clearly, sociopaths are in a league of their own, but acknowledging that someone close to you is only superficially charming takes a lot away from the relationship.

Add the sociopath's use of **charm** to his authoritarian persuasiveness and his strident glibness, and the pattern becomes obvious. But wisely the sociopath works at manipulating those he believes he can reel in. These characteristics seemed to inherently spill from both brothers. Admittedly, without a textbook or professional advice, fewer onlookers would have recognized either brother's tendency to be charmingly detrimental. Hold on, as the facts accumulate their history speeds forward

For example, Kiona Price, a Kingston waitress who partyied with them as early as 1991, believes "Rocky and Leon are real smart," basing that belief on her insistence that Leon attended Roane State Community College. She said she had only good things to say about them, and believed they had endured years of harassment both locally and nationally. A friend to the end, she invited anyone who would listen to a somewhat common Houston portrayal. Then she disappeared from her workplace and apparently Roane County. Attempts to contact her and her associates failed.

According to other friends to the Houstons, asking to be unnamed, they were saviors to their fan club: These sources said that the Houstons seemed real smart to their followers because of their capability to file lawsuits and recognize conspiracy in the highest levels of government. Amidst the group, the Houstons stood heads above their peers. They couldn't understand why some people were blind to the brothers Houston's messages. The two were working to save a nation that had "gone to the dogs."

Smaller and quieter segments said the Houstons were those dogs, but "wild dogs let loose." So waiting for what was sure to happen just continued.

One such man remembers being with friends when Rocky butted in as they casually gathered outside a food establishment. He immediately got up in one guy's face with his cocky questions. According to the source, "the man had no couth" and always seemed fixing for a fight. According to this source, the targeted man just excused himself and walked away. That is how Rocky "did people." No one wanted to mess around with him.

Such performances unmask another piece of the psychotherapist's understanding: Sociopaths have **no empathy** for others. Here again, anyone who invades a group of almost strangers in an attempt to spike up their emotions has a problem, probably more than one. Red flags fly. Both brothers invaded others privacy, and thought they were right doing so.

Pat Fultz Honeycutt, said to be Leon's girlfriend, instead publicly supported Leon's capacity for compassion. She spoke of his kindness towards strangers. Textbooks say sociopath's harbor a superficial intent to manipulate those they influence. If he intended to manipulate her with the random acts of kindness, she didn't see it that way.

Spending any time with their multiple lawsuits would prove their conspiracy theories daft. How any one of their followers could believe that the brothers Houston knew closely held national secrets remains a mystery. Those reverberating claims only spoke of **paranoia** and yelled out **grandiosity**.

If there was just criminal intent, then it turned on the tyrannical characteristics defined by Dr. Hare. But was there a leader and a follower? Did one so influence the other as to take him onto a treacherous path? Knowing the brothers were inseparable may explain the question. Perhaps one effectively did manipulate the other. The whole theoretical stage play seems now to have been told and acted out in front of a large part of East Tennessee. When adding the verbal outbursts, the pretentious self-importance, the missing behavior controls, the blame game, the paranoia, the tyrannical authoritarianism, and the general lack of empathy (or remorse), Rocky and Leon Houston were "not as nice as some people want to believe," says an observer who knew them well but who safely declined to be named.

Holding those in contempt who wanted to intercede points right back to Jack Stockton. Stockton's campaign that spring to become the Roane County Sheriff must have worried them, and perhaps been an ingredient in their motivation to kill and take control. Over the year's they had not been able to manipulate him. He looked electable.

Rocky, from what is seen in court documents, was referred to several psychiatrists who apparently didn't deem him a danger to others. Still, while professionals gave no statements on either man's ability to inflict harm nor turned over deteriorating mental health evaluations, common sense saw it. Plenty of witnesses knew they were dangerous men, whether they were simply "mean" or "crazy." Since the Houston clan was tighter than tight none of this would have set well with the closed cultish group.

The prediction was valid: Rocky Houston's rhetorical outburst in traffic court when faced with a fine forecast a storm: He was double trouble. Revealing his **grandiose** nature, he gave an extemporaneous outburst true only to a villain. Sharp people caught it: his message alerted his psychopathic proclivity. Stage center, he let slip the "all knowing and all powerful" self. Yet, presenting part of Dr. R. Hare's "sociopathic package" and that of other behavioral social scientists was never touched upon. The Houstons continued to remain more vaudevillians than villains. Those who heard and acknowledged the Waco threat and personal threat on the judge and his family stayed focused over the next five years, even though they took flak from the smaller community for harassing the two. It would have been difficult to miss the continuation of Rocky's and Leon's anti-government fever, which often had gone to a high alert.

Hind sight is clear vision. At this time, the Houston brothers only appeared to pose a serious threat to those directly involved in the judicial system. But it appears that the brothers, and others who make headlines, did send out these **clues**: They wanted to be noticed. Few could miss them as they pestered the courts and the press.

They got attention alright as they willingly exposed their intent to kill to unsuspecting listeners. Their pre-meditated testimonies went out to those they cornered: "They probably would have to kill some cops." That gets attention. Brought into court after the fact, that evidence could put pre-meditated murder before a jury.

Circumstances indicated that they intended to stand behind such "killings." They were hard to miss in their action character outfits. One man said, "every since I knew them, they wore body armor." And back in their immediate community their other choice of camouflage outer wear was passed off as a hunter's garb. Sporting it wasn't just a game.

Even though the behavior accelerated, it was not new to old school mates. Way back, people who once sat in classrooms alongside the Houstons' heard about those people who were "out to get them." Although altogether their **arrest records** were lean—actually another prevailing characteristic in independent studies of sociopaths by both Dr. Rhodes and Dr. Hare—close to home no one missed their reputation as "bad asses" and saw Leon over the years grow a reputation as a local "drug dealer."

Listening to friends talk about their gentle nature might have fooled a few. The self important, **narcissistic** person identified with sociopathy presents sympathic rebuttals to followers in order to help him earn and keep support. Rebut they did while manipulating their home-based audiences. They became wizards at stage management.

Others at school said that Rocky used his hot temper to bully other kids and, when he could, to intimidate teachers. In a Jekyll and Hyde manner the men drew followers, announced precursors to apocalyptic events, and promised parents a survivalist path to follow which would save the country for their children.

Chapter 33

Trained to Kill

Rocky Joe's Oak Ridge job was a significant one. For fifteen years he guarded the United States Department of Energy's nuclear facilities there. During those fifteen years, and according to area standards, he was well paid. At work he proudly carried a "Q" clearance (security required for high level government nuclear access); and he was "trained to kill," so law enforcement sources say who knew the job requirements.

Then, in 2003, that fifteen year career ended quickly. Houston's maniacal 2001 court room incident and many acts of criminally defiant behavior sealed it. In due course, his promises to judges, law enforcement, and his employer to get things turned around habitually had gone bad. Thumbing his nose at warrants added up. He wasn't hiding out in another state. He was right down the road smirking at all of them. This behavior, attached to his published anarchist's point of view, couldn't be overlooked.

Wackenhut, the U.S. arm of worldwide Group 4 Securicor, must have used unusual restraint during his employment with them. For example, talk has it that Rocky would sneak off to chat with a lawyer or two. That love-hate relationship with attorneys was quizzical.

Meanwhile those assigned to bring him in had a riskier job. They must have been uneasy as well. It was a no win situation: if successful they ran the risk of public criticism and loss of their jobs; and, if they were unsuccessful, they could end up dead.

The local law must have wondered just how much of either scenario lay in wait for them. While the Houston men talked about taking apart the government, authorities had to take a look at the possibility that the duo might take down a couple of them as well. Rocky pushed for an endgame. Accompanied by his usual high level of agitation, Mr. R. took his battle up a notch. His accomplice Leon always would be there for him. Clyde Houstons' boys saw the world their way. It was definitely different.

How could it be that Rocky kept his employment? During the years, watching the brothers' infamy rise, those at home settled on quiet supposition: Surly Wackenhut had known something of their employee's anti-government attacks. Neither he nor Leon ever seemed to hide much of it. Somehow secure in their sedition, they huffed and puffed about their First Amendment rights. Knowledgeable listeners knew those rights did not include assailing government with anarchists' messages. Just who could believe that the most vocal of the twosome guarded a national fortress which produced nuclear weapons components and government secrets?

Hired on to carry a formative weapon for one of the country's most secure facilities must have puffed up Rocky's pride and manliness. Guns do that somehow—with the exception of women whose gun ownership seldom changes their self-worth. Those who knew Rocky agreed that his attitude grew. If only in small proportions at first, bravado accompanied Rocky's security job at the Y-12 plant.

Part of the Oak Ridge complex is in Roane County, although most of Roane is a few miles south of the location known to the world. A large piece of history was made there. For a longtime it was top secret history (probably still is)! In fact the city was built around a special project, later found to be the uranium enrichment facilities of the Manhattan Project.

For years Oak Ridge was a closed city, off limits to everyone but workers. Now, museums and textbooks acknowledge its importance: the atomic bomb's uranium was produced on that the site. The workplace was innocuously named Y-12 then, and still is. This vast laboratory has shifted from this past to a new scientific presence. It remains a hub of worldwide recognition. The complex undertakings of the facility are central to the merging sciences that protect and benefit the lives Americans know and enjoy.

Overnight, Rocky Houston's rough homespun reputation changed from that of a farmer and farm boy at Midway High to a man the government trusted. Fairly so, anyone looking on now can feel the younger brother's ride: Known "back when" to classmates by that nickname "dirt," the man's job definitely added a shine to his shoes, money to his pockets, and status to his strut. He seems to have remained true to his country background and never took off to leave Leon or family behind.

Those who superficially knew him as a likeable security guard immediately noticed when Rocky was without his weapon. Suddenly his new assignment seemed to be "patrolling the parking lot." It sounds as if his workplace life had turned to probationary. According to onlookers, he didn't lose anytime making his situation worse.

By 2003, and out of a job at Y-12, Rocky Joe Houston stepped up his second career choice for fulfillment. He had filed multiple others lawsuits before, but perhaps with less speed and repetitiveness. And so with added vengeance, Mr. R.J. Houston filed his first lawsuit of 2003 in Knoxville's Federal Court on January 10th.

His self-drawn paper work must have attracted no more or no less than the usual attention. Houston lawsuits, most often personally crafted, were well known at this level of the justice system: He was and had remained a regular litigant there—even after the incarceration on the felony murder charges.

The most damaging insights and details about his security work, as reported under the coveted cloak of anonymity, actually came from friendly faces. Those familiar with the younger Houston brother recognized him on sight at the Oak Ridge installation and had occasional conversations with him. None seemed to know him well but remember that "he was a real hoot." They liked the guy who they knew on a one-dimensional basis, but were uncomfortable with personal information he settled on them.

A middle-aged woman in an administrative position there was one of these people. She remembers being truly surprised when she learned of his alleged crime. Others were not surprised at all. Uncomfortably they all looked back and came forth with knowledge they wanted to deliver without repercussion: They feared that forfeiting Houston information could cause them trouble—the dangerous kind.

Rocky, according to those who would listen to him, told people at work about a Houston armory on his farm in that South of the [Tennessee] River community at Ten Mile. He boasted of enough ammunition on their property to support a standoff. He also proudly pictured this arsenal protected by bunkers somewhere beyond the pastures and within the mountain ranges of their property lines.

Cave openings do dot the area's mountain curvatures. Such entrances pop up among the scenic flora and rocks along Roane County's hair pin turns and back roads, Many private properties South of the River, and on farther to Chattanooga claim similar topography.

Right there Civil War soldiers left remnants of their lives. Right there Roane's trenches and caves speak significantly of America's divided losses. Righteous warriors settled down with their own small fires, put out bed rolls, rested and ate before moving onto Chattanooga. They marched on to battles at Chickamauga, Missionary Ridge, and Lookout Mountain. Many met their deaths in what also was a government showdown.

As a point of fact, a city employee had reported the same "bunker" information to Kingston officials. But no one ever got close enough to take a "look see." To those familiar with the boundaries of the Houston properties, these boasts made more sense than nonsense. They also felt that particular bunker would not be found without assistance. If it existed, no one was willing to sign up for that hunting expedition. They definitely had been asked to volunteer.

Chapter 34

Smoking Them Out

A fire brought on the final episode of those fifteen years of push and shove between the family and government. Volunteer fire personnel sighted a fire on the Houston property and reported it. The Tennessee Forestry Department sent their people to put it out. As the account was given, Rocky and Leon, with guns pointed ran off the "government" help. Some in the fire tower swear they saw those boys "over there laughing about it." Were they setting up those fire fighters as they may have set up the men in the marked county patrol car?

Perhaps they shrewdly plotted a forestry department face off. And if witnesses to this are to be believed, they set a fire and waited. The Tennessee Forestry Department arriving to look down the wrong end of Houston rifle barrels smartly left. Their idea of an evitable government tango did not go off that day but had been given birth.

The brothers Houston then put out their own fire. A warrant was taken out. Apparently the warrant remained outstanding. From there, it would appear that they eventually got what they wanted: they tangled with the law and the law lost.

Could it be that the Houstons believed even before the killings that they could eventually mount a creative defense that no one would live to witness against? They definitely had plenty of time on their hands to concoct all kinds of scenarios.

Then too, there were many bystanders to figuratively fan the flames of even this small fire. Plenty of people there and nationwide romanticize such dangerous behaviors. They see it as "outlaw cool." The likes of them would never "rat" on their heroes. No, they would wait for additional entertainment.

Richard Rhodes, criminal justice specialist and author of *Why They Kill*, addresses that same subject with a recommendation: "people in general should read violent crime in order to prevent them from romanticizing their perpetrators." A little bit of knowledge, known as "a dangerous thing," seems to be what supported the long going Houston saga. More knowledgeable folks never would have believed them to be courageous patriots or excitingly cool. "Perps," (those who perpetuate crime) they had been and "perps" they were.

Their game of hit and run played well until the end. It must have entertained them as it did some followers.

Chapter 35

Government in Their Sights

Even early in 2000 the disturbing duo grew a list of targeted "conspirators" to include incredible reaches. Such auspicious hopes included Tennessee Governor Phil Bredesen and President George Bush. No questions linger here: they wanted people to believe they had enemies in high places.

Known for their epic erratic behavior, the East Tennessee press labeled the Roane County men the "anti-government brothers." Their names entered the public domain, and, as they did, they became a brand name of sorts. Wrapped in their outlandish continuing past and present, the "boys" forged ahead. They had no doubts; no regrets. Indeed, they continued to feed off their "big shot" approach to bad.

In some ways they brought about a coup d'état: Always fronting as victims, they put themselves on equal ground with those they accused. They climbed from obscurity into some fierce limelight. From nobodies to some bodies, they and their shadowy associates initiated personal challenges against governing bodies.

As reported here, their beliefs were similar to a variety of cult groups seen as domestic terrorists. The Posse Commitatus of the 80's and 90's acted as loosely bound groups of government agitators. They refused to recognize any part of the United States government that they could not control. Often that simply came down to county governments where their faithful lived.

Somehow the Houston behavior throughout the 90's and until 2006 looked awfully similar: These two men and the Posse continually went after the sheriff; they participated in "paper terrorism," sending hundreds of subpoenas across the country; they shamelessly shouted out conspiracy theories; they attempted to handcuff a judge; and they constantly worked to intimidate law enforcement with their threats. Finally, they often talked about violent ends as these two dead men provided for them. But they were never brave, bold, or as bad as they believed. The Houstons did not wait to encounter the parade of law enforcement coming down Highway 58 following the shooting. They ran!

The explicit Commitatus handbook theoretically took on the local sheriff. Their goal was to kill him if he wasn't cooperative. The Feds put a lid on most of them back then. Of course, if they operate undercover today, they would have ditched the name(s) used then for a surreptitious one(s).

Among the analysts then who attacked this behavior, the phrase "saving the country for your children" became a cliché. Information exists to point out that the Houstons used the line as if they had a copyright on it. These two high school graduates known as "Dirt" and "Crash" in 1978and 1979 at Midway High were leading alright, but not as the country's saviors.

On the other hand their political message did not yet boast a kiss of death. The necessity to "kill a cop," according to those who knew them to say it, evolved over time. Any criminal psychology text acknowledges that most criminal behavior edges upward with time. If killing an uncooperative sheriff could be a self-styled initiation into the Posse Commitatus thinking, then accomplishing such an article of faith might be a goal. And, if it couldn't be the sheriff then why not a sheriff's deputy?

To track the behavior, one could go back even to the early '90's: At that time Clifford Leon voiced United States Constitutional ideology when he skirmished with law enforcement. Television had become somewhat of a mass communication weapon. Perhaps changing times and changing people advanced the thinking of law breakers. Conceivably 24 hour television, introduced by the Cable News Network in the 80's and influential by the 90's, made conduct once taboo more accepted: Crimes started to appear some what common place and materialize everywhere at once. If you decided to be bad, perhaps you felt you were not alone. Purposely the Ten Mile two leaped on others' espoused anti-government thinking. Their ancestral tree now buried on Houston property might have shaken a few leaves in embarrassment. But Rocky and Leon went on. If they had felt ashamed of their game, they would have stopped long prior to their final act.

By 1995 most Americans knew all about the horrific bombing of Oklahoma City's Alfred P. Murrah Federal Building. Domestic demons killed only innocents at that nightmarish scene. Suddenly a beef with the government meant blood loss for children and ordinary citizens in what became their tomb.

Separatists' perpetrators Timothy McVeigh and Terry Nichols were convicted. McVeigh was executed on June 11, 2001. Of course just three months later on Sept. 11, 2001 nearly 3,000 people died at the World Trade Center in New York. Then too, May 11 marks the deaths of Jones and Brown. Talk about "crazies" and conspiracy theories. Linking dates might make as much sense as linking the number of dollar bills in your pocket. Some people have mad trivia games that the rest of us never will understand. Yet, the Oklahoma anger was more commonly linked to the Waco deaths. At the time it couldn't be missed. The brothers Houston, according to those who heard them, had spouted off similar Waco viewpoints. And Rocky's Waco threats couldn't be downplayed even though a jury seemed to have been convinced to do so.

Conceivably the Houstons' diatribe didn't get the result they wanted; or perhaps, in fact, it did get that result. Unfortunately their immediate and continuing reputation generally remained overlooked. They were humorously ignorant to those who heard of them but didn't deal with them. Asked to explain, people could better compare the law's problems with the Houstons to television scripts for "Andy of Mayberry." In those episodes, Sheriff Andy Taylor appeared to have similar problems with the disruptive hillbilly Ernest T. Bass. Wouldn't Ernest have attempted to arrest and handcuff Circuit Court Judge Russell Simmons during a courtroom proceeding? How wrong such conjecture would have been.

When court jesters take over courtrooms, citizens need to awaken. Without the rule of law, communities become so jeopardized that only wild men rule. But were the Houstons just "idiots," as the mother of the deceased victim Mike Brown called them, or had they cleverly joined the ideology of other underground splinter groups? For a fact, tracking circumstantial evidence from beginning to end of the Houston nightmare shows over and over how other groups talked the talk in lawsuits and at home. They and the Houstons recused lawyers and judges, charged fraud and conspiracy, got news headlines, and pursued a path that posted accumulated stacks of paper throughout the court system—the purpose being to waylay its efficiency.

Behaving like cult copycats, they were far from unique. Certainly repeated facts bear their enthusiasm for parallel activities. Those militant extremists actively involved in domestic terrorism for years have patched together an ideological quilt that offers plenty of inclusion. They often belong to groups that believe disparate ideas. They simply join together in a coalition of hate.

Varying dogma has included those groups already addressed here as well as white supremacists, anti-abortion opponents, Puerto Rican separatists, environmentalist, animal rights activists, tax evaders, religious sects, and of course those involved in bombing the Oklahoma City federal building April 19, 1995. According to the Southern Poverty Law Center, 168 were killed and 500 injured there. Interestingly, the Center in Montgomery, Alabama Center also reports at least fifteen law enforcement officers have been killed since by such domestic terrorists.

Such terrorists' forces grow substantially as these allegiances stretch beyond their own causes. That growth and camaraderie creates a more masterful effort to obstruct justice. The threat levels consequently raise proportionately against their law enforcement and government enemies. In order: nihilists' seeds are sewn and commingle with other groups—even those who are dissimilar. Targeting the United States Government from within becomes their commonality.

With the help of the internet these quarrelsome groups clandestinely market the growth of their philosophical products. Due to upgraded internet surveillance, some anti-government groups go on the sly beneath the radar by switching to the use of almost forgotten short wave radios. Such furtive connections build hidden networks.

Outsiders do not see it happening. And towns cannot and do not police these circumstances, leaving the scrutiny to state and federal agencies. The most recent example must be that of the self-appointed Mormon "prophet" Warren Jeffs' polygamist compound in Texas. It took the state and federal government to act against the long known lawbreakers. National news portrayed the local surrounding governments as knowing what went on and living with it.

Outside support could not be denied or proven in the case of the tempestuous brothers. Witnesses do report that Rocky Houston expressed an above average interest in internet skills, which by itself does not convict him of anything. More and more Americans use electronic messaging. But, his interest in developing specialty knowledge, as indicated by more than a few who came forward, could throw light on the possibility of Houston ties to anti-government others.

Examples of such exposed extremist support frequently surfaces. The Associated Press's Holly Ramer cites an example in her syndicated 2007 news piece: A tax evading couple attracted unwanted press by accumulated help from a huge number of militant sympathizers across the country. The couple had been arrested for hiding $1.9 million dollars in income in order to avoid federal taxes. Instead of facing trial on these charges, the anti-government, anti-tax husband and wife fled to their home and acreage.

The hide-and-seek game is common to such radicals. Somehow anti-government individuals align on protocol. They boldly invite a war. This couple literally stood their ground on their 100 acre New Hampshire property.

A major misstep drew the unwanted attention: Large numbers of strangers began to visit the well fortified encampment. Neighbors called in their growing suspicions, and in so doing, they exposed their subversive network. Ancillary militiamen and anti-government sympathizers often had swarmed the property, giving moral and financial support to the couple. Picnic style gatherings alerted federal authorities who slyly took their own picnic provisions to gain access to the property where they arrested the duo.

Again Houston similarities cannot be missed. They played hide-and-seek with the law, gathered more than enough support from outsiders, and threatened to shoot it out if confronted. To add to the similarities, the New Hampshire family had gone into a survivalist mode by placing weapons, ammunition and homemade bombs inside and outside of their house. And so the Tennessee nightmare developed and grew over time, as days developed into years in Roane County.

Separately, Rocky and Leon Houston's finances leave questions. Large expenses went into their Houston and Houston legal charade: one mailing of federally stamped subpoenas cost them $300 dollars. Expensive guns and ammunition seemed abundant. Lawyers were hired and fired. And only a few immediate family members drew regular paychecks.

Logically, the Houstons may have gone beyond their little corner of the world for sustenance and financial support. And although there was Houston land, rumors of large debt encumbering it swept Ten Mile.

Even if they never had talked to or read about other anti-government "patriots," they knew the drills. According to Roane law enforcement, one officer who had "gained entry" into Rocky Houston's home described "guns at every window" and miscellaneous body armor strategically located.

As with most militant groups, the Houstons had promised violence. For a fact, no preacher would again talk them down as Pastor Paul Lloyd did when he entered Rocky's barricaded house to bring him in while law enforcement stood by. Their behavior assured a violent ending to anyone who came after them next time. Such revolutionary Houston choices must have played hard in law circles as they witnessed the heroic attention given to Rocky and Leon. The Ten Mile two had built a fan base from some people they never would know, but who relished such battles from the distant sidelines.

But close associates there were. A Houston friend with children behaved similarly. He was tight with the Houstons and tried to sabotage his own warrant by taking cover on the Houston property. He had repeatedly threatened to kill a man and his daughter, and the man wanted him arrested. Warrants were taken out and a joint city and county operation brought him into the jail. In that case, with the cooperation of Sheriff Haggard, they sent an unidentified vehicle with SWAT members hidden within. They picked him up and no one died.

Rocky's house (independent of the homestead, but only yards away on Barnard Narrows) was also home to his wife and teenage children. This is the house Rocky ran to when he resisted the law. These fearful risks he laid on family members never seemed to slow him down or stop him.

The brothers Houston's battle, right or wrong, continued according to plan for over a decade. Other anarchist groups and the Houstons used "frivolous lawsuits" to overload and bring down the court system. They claimed themselves harassed although they were informed harassers. They stalked government with nonsense in an attempt to intimidate the justice system. Their bottom line goal, according to authorities, was to establish minimalist individual governments close to their bases. That beginning and ending, according to such known premises, depended on their ability to control the local government. If they could not control them, it was thought they should "take them out" by some manner or means.

With or without help the Houstons continued to casually play havoc with good government. Perhaps they merged their thoughts with other national conspirators: Surely, there was intent when they began way back to mailing each printed complaint with personal handwritten postscripts. The addendums actually read as retaliatory lightning bolts hidden in propaganda. In saying that they "feared," they also insinuate that they should have an option of a first strike. In essence their "fear" would prove them innocent when they killed any one of their named conspirators. No one could deny that they were crafty guys.

Citing their constitutional rights as their practiced agenda moved forward, they themselves set the clock for the countdown. Such behavior, even when cloaked in nonsense, lives until it is stopped. In their case the nightmare ate away at the community, until Jones and Brown died while "outing" them as killers. Astutely the co-dependent brothers lived through their performance.

Chapter 36

Nightmare Speeds On

The early Waco threat sent out emotional ice cycles. Rocky's warning in 2001 emerged as predictable. It still meant waiting, especially after a local jury acquitted him later for his threat. But beneath the surface, the nightmare speeds on.

Those weapons added up too. Again and again the brothers Houston brandished them. They talked big about a close-to-home arsenal. And their bunker mentality and militia-styled appearances substantiated the duos "come after me" confidence. Such a heated profile carries weight. All the time the two were writing their own script in blood.

The Waco warning stands stone cold. At this exact point those years of anti-government remarks take a turn for the worse. With his loud mouth the animated Rocky puts on the pressure of an abusive spouse and raises the alert level. Possibility becomes probability.

That code red step also had accompanied the Waco cult's probabilities. United States Attorney Janet Reno believed a large cache of illegal assault rifles fortified the charismatic cult leader David Karash's Texas compound. As predicted, it was found to be true.

Predictably the man remained self-righteous. He couldn't hold his mouth when the local jury absolved his Waco threat behavior. Predictably he ranted about their decision to charge him with disorderly conduct. How relieved and grateful he should have been. Perhaps the jury members' decision had been conditioned by the fear that always accompanied the fanatic Houston.

Yes, the county's citizens recognized the bad to the bone para-military behavior. They also knew the duos camouflage and road blocks had nothing to do with hunting seasons. Barnard Narrows looked more like death camp than deer camp. It was safer to look away.

Twisting every action, to include the escape from sentencing at his "Waco trial," he took charge again. Predictably it gave Rocky Joe a larger criminal future. His acquittal moved onto the probability that the brothers Houston would eventually unveil the rest of the nightmare. Without question, the timeline following the acquittal escalated to revenge and murder.

Seventh District Constable Butch Barding had long before let his mind go beyond the possibility to probability. He had been close to the Houstons and the "county law." Knowing as well as anyone the predictability and the probability of what lie in wait, he knew the long lasting nightmare had exploded. Instinctively as he heard the gaggle of sirens rushing down Highway 58, he knew the inevitable had come about. Coming toward him as they crossed the river toward his own home just a distance from Barnard Narrows, he knew. "Oh my," it must be the Houstons and the law.

Country people in East Tennessee are reticent by nature and taught to close-up when strangers come asking questions. People were as tight lipped about the Houstons following their first-degree murder charges as they had been before. Regional lore supports the cultural trait.

Today crowds cheer and sing mountain lyrics with respect for the past. To them it is the tradition of a state that stands strong in individuality, pride, self-reliance and yes even once illegal problem solving.

Chapter 37

Post Script

The nightmare that for years had held minds in place and emotions on edge lay like low-lying storm clouds while legal motions and legal moves worked up to the possibility of long awaited trials. But the infinite nature of time could change things. But the community knows inside of its privately held fear that lawlessness may march on.

This analysis and this story end with two trials waiting: one for Leon Houston and another for Rocky Houston. The book went forward into the publication process in June. No trials yet had occurred. But if nightmares teach, then many people should learn and profit from all of this, with the exception of Jones and Brown.

"Lying in wait" within this book is only applied to idiomatic nightmares and not specifically to the legal charge which implies the premeditation or malice aforethought necessary for first degree murder. All such charges are left to the justice system and the decision of a jury. The nightmares referred to in ordinary conversation are those discussed within this piece of "literary journalism." Such dark moments that many East Tennessee citizens experienced can last for a week or years. They keep an individual or a body of people on edge. It is fearfully haunting to know something will happen but not know when or where. That destructive knowledge, concealed by criminal minds that abide its existence, lie in wait: There they forcefully weaken the resolve of those who oppose their sinister direction. And so it has been with the Houstons of Roane County; and so it will be as the whole East Tennessee community awaits two trials and two results.

Importantly, in America a person is presumed innocent of a crime until proven guilty. This does not mean that the person(s) is innocent when brought to trial. He would not be on trial if the justice system had not already determined that the accused may have committed a crime. Jurors are directed to find a defendant not guilty if in their minds they hold a reasonable doubt as to the guilt of the accused. The procedure gives the defense and the accused that benefit of a doubt.

##########

Bibliography

"Brandenburg," http://en.wikipedia.org/wiki/Brandenburg_v._Ohio
Accessed March 7,2008

Bryant, Felicia Bryant who with her husband wrote "Rocky Top."
Accessed October 20, 2006

FBI "Terror," http://www.fbi.gov/publications/terror/terror99.pdf
Accessed November 24, 2006

"Freemen," http://en.wikipedia.org/wiki/Montana_Freemen
Accessed January 17, 2007

Hare, Robert D., Ph.D.
http://www.geocities.com/lycium7/hare-checklist.html
Accessed November 8, 2007

"Harriman," http://en.wikipedia.org/wiki/Harriman,_Tennessee
Accessed June 16, 2007

Historic Roane County Courthouse Heritage Commission
Accessed November 3, 2006

"Jeffs,Warren," http://desertnews.com/dn/view/o,1249,645197023,00
Html
Accessed May 30, 2008

"Manhattan Project," Wikipedia,
http://en.wikipedia.org/wiki/Oak_Ridge,_Tennessee
Accessed June 17, 2008

"McVeigh"
http://archives.cnn.com/2001/LAW/06/11/mcveigh.02/index.html
Accessed December 10,2006

"Military Extremists in the United States"
http://www.cfr.org/publication
Accessed May 8, 2006

"Posse-Comitatus,"
http://www.nizkor.org/hweb/orgs/american/adl/paranoia-as-
/adl/paranoia-as-patriotism/posse-comitatus.htm
Accessed April 10, 2007

"Tennessee History," http://www.tennesseehistory.com/class/
.Alamo.htm
Accessed May 12, 2008

"T.V.A.", http://www.answers.com/topic/tennessee-valley- http.:///
Search.yahoo.com/?p=TVA+eminent+domain+in+Union+County
Accessed July 19, 2007

"Wackenhut,"http://en.wikipedia.org/wiki/Wackenhut
Accessed April 27, 2007

"Waco," http://www.rickross.com/groups/waco.html
Accessed August 13, 2007

"Y-12," http://www.y12.doe.gov/
Accessesd February 21, 2007

About the Author

Babette began her career at the CBS Network, Atlanta. She has written for newspapers, state and national officials, and published the award-winning "A War to Safeguard Students as Citizens." She also was invited to participate in "Writing and Reading for Civic Education" at Harvard University. As a University of Florida and Citadel graduate, she avidly follows college sports and swims a mile each day at the local YMCA.

Printed in the United States
152265LV00006B/27/P